ARCHIE "GUNSLINGER" COOLEY

THE MAKING OF A FOOTBALL LEGEND

DARRYL C. GAINES AND JOHN M. BRANSON III

FOREWORD BY ALBERT G. EDWARDS

Copyright © 2019 by Darryl Gaines

All rights reserved. No part of this publication may be reproduced, distributed, or transmitted in any form or by any means, including photocopying, recording, or other electronic or mechanical methods, without the prior written permission of the publisher, except in the case of brief quotations embodied in critical reviews and certain other noncommercial uses permitted by copyright law.

ISBN-13: 978-1-970079-60-9

Published and edited by:
Opportune Independent Publishing Co.
113 N. Live Oak Street
Houston, TX 77003
(832) 263-1700
www.opportunepublishing.com

TABLE OF CONTENTS

INTRODUCTION	**7**
FOREWORD	**15**
TRAINING UP A CHILD	**19**
Growing up in the Segregated South	19
High School, the Journey Begins	24
THE TIGER YEARS	**27**
Football	27
In the Center of it All	30
Baseball	32
Love at First Sight	33
A SEMI-PRO BASEBALL PLAYER	**37**
The Laurel Black Cats	37
A LEGEND IN THE MAKING	**39**
From Player to Coach	39
Plans Interrupted	39
SERVING HIS COUNTRY	**41**
A Military Jock	41
THE VALLEY YEARS	**47**
A Recruiting Genius	50
The Architect of the Spread and No Huddle Offense	52
Training Camp	58

Practice in the "Hideaway" … 59
"TONs of FUN" … 62
A Nation in Awe … 72
The "Game of the Century" … 82
The Playoffs … 87
SWAC Domination … 89
The Red Devils … 90
Red Devils Offense … 91
Red Devils Defense … 94
Athletic Directors, Trainers, Sports Writers … 96

TRAINERS … 99
Equipment … 99
Medical … 100
NFL Knocking at the Door … 100

AFTER THE VALLEY … 103
EPILOGUE … 111
STATS … 113
Cooley has a rich and broad coaching background … 115
AWARDS … 115
PHOTO GALLERY … 117
MEMORIAL … 117
Players and Fans … 118
CONTRIBUTORS … 143

INTRODUCTION

Archie "Gunslinger" Cooley and Mohamad Ali

Webster's dictionary defines a legend as "one who inspires." I would add to this description words like, "great," "genius," and "giant" to fully color the image and importance of the story you are about to read and the man you are about to meet. Archie "Gunslinger" Cooley stands today as one of the greatest Southwestern Athletic Conference (SWAC) football coaches in the history of Historically Black Colleges and Universities (HBCU) football.

A genius playmaking architect and giant along with his peers Eddie Robinson, Marino Casem, and Joe Gibson. He continues to be recognized by former NFL coaches and players, sports enthusiasts, sports announcers and writers. He receives heartfelt recognition and honor from those who graduated from SWAC universities, for his accomplishments and the attention his success brought to the SWAC, the Mississippi Delta, and Mississippi Valley State University.
Cooley was a formidable force, with a charismatic and confident personality. He had a knack for convincing players to trust in each other, do what he told

them, believe in his plan, and fight like hell to the very end. In return, he would show them what victory looked like on the other side. Cooley was true to his word, as history records him as the winningest head coach at Mississippi Valley State University. He recruited Jerry Rice and Willie Totten, as well as a host of football players from around the country, to assemble a winning Delta Devils football team.

He did not care where his players came from or what their status was. He was not afraid to walk into homes in low-income neighborhoods to recruit and give a young player an opportunity to join his team. He just believed he could give any player a vision, prepare him for the game and he would be on his way to victory. He was developing boys who would become men of honor, integrity, and character, and he did it well. He put them through a program he had developed and tested over the years as he was learning and being mentored himself.

His program pushed his players to their limits, as it required them to learn how to lead and depend on each other. It turned them into a close-knit brotherhood of soldiers, which they themselves deemed each other "Red Devils" after making it through Cooley's gauntlet of grueling early morning, afternoon, and late evening practice sessions and film study. Cooley still wears his cowboy hat and is as charismatic and confident as he was while still coaching. Many of his former players and coaches to this day continue to visit and communicate with him for advice, as he remains a beloved coach and mentor.

To begin I'd like to first tell the story behind the cowboy hat and nickname. It all starts with Roscoe Nance, sports reporter for the Jackson Daily News, who visited Mississippi Valley to write a story on the Delta Devils and saw Cooley at practice wearing a straw mailman-type hat. With an eye for flare, he suggested to Cooley that he wear it all the time. Cooley thought, "Maybe I will," but in true Cooley fashion, he had to raise the stakes. He got himself a fancy grey cowboy hat. Cooley liked the hat and his new look and wore the hat during his first game as a head coach against Morris Brown. It was also his first victory in his new role as a head coach, and he remembers everyone going crazy about this coach with the cowboy hat.

During the post-game press conference, several reporters made comments about his hat, telling him how much they liked it. It was a big hit so Cooley decided he would wear it from then on for every game. Roscoe was not done with his suggestions yet, and said to Cooley, "You need a nickname now." He said, "Even Head Coach Marino Casem has a nickname, 'The Godfather,' and you need one too."

At that point, Cooley had established himself as a coach who was not afraid to throw the football, and he threw it a lot. Roscoe said, "You're a gunslinger, Cooley, throwing downfield without any hesitation." To that Cooley replied, "You're right! I'm not afraid of throwing against anybody. I like that name, Roscoe. When you write about me, use my nickname, 'Gunslinger!'" With his hat and nickname, Cooley had become a coach with distinction, and he set himself apart enforcing his strategy of preparing and outworking his opponents. This philosophy, along with his eye for talent, was a major factor in Cooley's success as a head coach.

Cooley at his best, describing victory

Introducing the Gunslinger is one of the greatest honors I have had in my life, as I take this opportunity to tell you about his life and how it all started; taking you on the journey as I saw it, participated in it, and experienced it. What you are about to read is a story about a man who, like me, came from humble beginnings. We both started out life in the projects and made our way through trials, tribulations, and uncertainty. Cooley, however, had to endure a much deeper environment of segregation and had to push past greater obstacles than I could ever imagine.

He created opportunity where it did not exist, and used what he had to make things work, even if it was not enough. Through it all, he remained vigilant, steadfast, and true. Cooley, through his efforts and determination, found his way to become the Gunslinger, the legendary cowboy hat wearing head coach of Mississippi Valley State University.

As a young and energetic kid from Mobile, Alabama, with a restless spirit and a never-ending desire to find life's next big challenge, I did not realize that the challenge was actually looking for me and Cooley was at the head of it. This challenge was ready to thrust me into a new world, to take me on a journey I could not have imagined for myself. I was about to cross paths with a soon-to-be legendary coach, a man of great courage, perseverance, and strength. Archie "Gunslinger" Cooley was about to become a major part of my life and direction.

This legendary coach was a man I was destined to meet, a man who would provide me with the challenges that would make me who I am today. He would raise my standing as a true student athlete to its highest point, finishing the groundwork toward my success that John L. Leflore high school in Mobile, Alabama, had started. Before graduating from Leflore High in 1983, I was blessed to have had all the opportunities I could manage.

I spent those years playing football, drums in the marching band, and taking magnet school classes in computers. I wanted to do everything I could, learn everything I could, and experience as much as I could. I was a sponge, unafraid and willing to try anything at least once. While playing football, I played both sides of the ball as a tight end on offense and a corner back and safety on defense, as well as a punter and kicker.

I had done well in football, earning several local awards and second team all-state honors. I had received letters of interest from Texas A&M, Georgia Tech, Purdue, and Michigan. Little did I know that none of the letters I received mattered one bit to the person who would decide my fate, my mother. Long before I thought I had a choice in the matter, she had already decided that she was sending me to Mississippi Valley State University. Neither my father nor I had ever met Coach Cooley, but before we knew it he had already run a coup on my family, and his plans were solid.

My mother did not even want to discuss the matter at all. She was completely uninterested in talking about it. No discussion, no thinking about it, no reasoning. When it came time to start visiting schools, I asked her about responding to requests to visit a few of the other schools and got a straightforward stare and stern voice in response. "You are going to Mississippi Valley State University." My heart sunk. It was as if I had already signed a contract that was non-negotiable. My father had given up on trying to convince her, which meant I was on my way to the Mississippi Delta, a place I had never heard of or knew anything about.

The Gunslinger

On signing day at Leflore High, I watched three of my teammates sign with Grambling while I was the lone signee with Mississippi Valley State, becoming one of Cooley's boys. In the midst of it all, there was one thing I knew for sure: God's plan is always the best plan. Little did I know he was including me in a magical journey, a movement, an experience that was on the horizon. I would be riding with the Delta Devil posse, with the legendary Gunslinger leading the way.

He would take my skills and talent and turn up the gain, push me to my limits, and then push some more, all while molding me into a strong willed and focused young man.

Cooley gave me the experiences, the knowledge, the confidence, and the desire to be a winner. He would teach me how to lead and reach deep within, how to push far beyond the sight of what I had envisioned for myself, then push some more. He gave me life skills, the fundamentals, and said, "Remember, when things go wrong, always go back to the basics." I, along with many others, owe Coach Cooley a great deal of gratitude for the impact he has had on our lives. He pushed us both athletically and academically.

I remember him saying, "You get your education Gaines, because I'm going to get my football out of you." He did just that from day one. He didn't mince words; he walked the walk and talked the talk. If you did not meet his expectations, he would cut you in a heartbeat and everyone knew it. He would always remind us, as he pushed us through some god-awful drill, yelling across the practice field so everyone could hear, "IT'S HARD BUT IT'S FAIR, GENTLEMAN!" I remember thinking, during one of our many non-stop running drills, "He is trying to kill us, and he is over there on the sideline enjoying this!" I had been through this a few times by now and was begrudgingly radicalized to never quit, so I kept moving along with everyone else. We were mesmerized by Cooley and hoped to survive long enough that he would get tired of watching the misery and anguish he was bestowing upon us.

Cooley gave me a toolbox of survival and leadership skills that provided me with what I needed to be successful and share with others toward their own success. When I hear him say to me how proud he is of what I have accomplished, it is heartfelt and it reminds me of the days he and I spent in the Delta, at Mississippi Valley State University, and how all the hard work he put me through contributed to who I am today.

The many skills I learned from him include taking responsibility for myself, engaging in teamwork and relationships, developing goals and preparing to attain them, maintaining attitude and gratitude, and outworking my opponent.

These are the skills I used when I was hired by McDonnell Douglas Aircraft as a software developer after graduating from Valley. And remember I told you that I was always looking for challenges? Well, another one came my way. I received a call to play in the National Football League (NFL) for the Kansas City Chiefs in 1988.

There was only one catch, I had already signed a contract with McDonnel Douglas Aircraft. In typical fashion, I was dead set on doing both, and God's favor showed up again when the Kansas City Chiefs and McDonnel Douglas Aircraft both agreed to allow me to play football and work during the off-season. It was truly a win-win-win scenario. Cooley had set me up for success, and the opportunity to play in the NFL and work at McDonnel Douglas were my victories and pushed me even further.

This scenario gave me the opportunity to use the skills I had learned on the testing grounds with Cooley in real-time, with actual application resulting in true, real-life responses and feedback. I found myself gainfully employed with the best of both worlds, and I owed Coach Cooley big-time.

Today, I am an executive at the National Aeronautics and Space Administration (NASA) where I work with engineers, scientists, and technical and administrative experts in space exploration. I have traveled the world, developed many relation-ships, and managed space programs and projects with great benefit for the nation. Daily, I use the skills Cooley provided me, as I manage projects, lead people, mentor and work through issues and concerns. It has been advantageous for me, especially in times of uncertainty, when I have had to dig deep down for my strength and direction. During those times, I have always recalled those words, "It's hard but it's fair."

Many times, I see others struggle with problems that I easily address, work through, and solve. I credit this ability to Cooley and all I learned from him in the "hideaway", the practice field at the far east corner of the Mississippi Valley State University campus. That field was a proving ground for Cooley and his football system. For me, it was a classroom, and the lessons I learned there work like a charm.

There are countless stories untold and memories unheard, of how the Gunslinger made his way to legendary status. His methods and systems were developed and honed over many years as he coached at all levels and in different sports arenas. His success affected and influenced the National Collegiate Athletic Association (NCAA) and the National Football League (NFL) simultaneously. He brought national attention to one of the smallest schools in the country, in the middle of the Mississippi Delta, in a little-known town called Itta Bena where Mississippi Valley State University is located. With a recruiting budget that most schools would spend in a day, he took what he was given and turned it into something the world of sports would pay close attention to.

It was with the greatest pleasure that I asked John M. Branson III, the well-known and revered Valley News editor-in-chief, to work alongside me to support and write about what we consider one of the greatest historical periods in sports. This period includes a man on a journey, a man who allowed us both to travel along and watch in awe as he became a legend. Although John and Cooley didn't see eye to eye on many topics at first, they had great respect for one another.

John didn't mince words, he called it as he saw it and Cooley, well, let's just say, didn't like what john said in his sports writings about what he saw. Today they both laugh at the past and all is well. John and I interviewed Cooley as well as his family members, former players, coaches, and others to capture special moments and thoughts about him. We begin where it all began for him, in Laurel, Mississippi. We end with a legend made, one who continues to be honored to this day by the National Collegiate Football Association.

This book will shed light on Cooley's life and things that most do not know about him. As he shared his knowledge and experiences with many of his players and coaches, we bring into focus those who advised and shared with him. He is truly a great man, a giant and a genius in the game of football and the game of life to so many. It is with the greatest honor that we bring forth this story for the world to know how a man, who was given so little, in turn produced and gave most abundantly. This book is not only a biography but also a tribute to Archie "Gunslinger" Cooley, the coach, the mentor, the legend.

FOREWORD

I have had the honor of knowing both the author, and co-author for well over 35 years. Darryl Gaines and I met during the summer of 1983, having recently graduated from High School in Mobile Alabama and electing to attend summer school at Mississippi Valley State University to get acclimated to the football program and college life.

Over the course of our freshman year, we became close friends, and even family, since those days, having shared many of life's most rewarding and challenging experiences together. Darryl first distinguished himself to the MVSU Family by making a proclamation that he would major in Computer Science, despite some concerns from the coaching staff of that day, about the strenuous requirements of the program, while participating and exceling in one of the most rigorous football programs in College Football.

Not only did Darryl excel on the football field, matriculating to play professionally with the Kansas City Chiefs, and later the Canadian Football League, but also as a business and technology executive, making a mark on space travel, while ensuring that young people are afforded the opportunity and benefits of facilitated exposure to Science, Technology, Engineering and Math (STEM) related educational programs. Many of us prefer to study problems before making a commitment, Darryl on the other hand follows his heart, and figures out what is required afterwards. This is why it is so appropriate that he is the man to document the life of one of College Football's most revolutionary and impactful coach, Archie "The Gunslinger" Cooley.

John M. Branson, III affectionately known as "John Boy" contributed to this chapter of history from an entirely different perspective. John befriended Carl Binder, also a native of Mobile Alabama, who started out as a football player, but had the rare talent to change sports at the collegiate level to become a starting power forward on MVSU's Basketball Team, also a history making squad of this generation. Carl introduced John to Darryl and I, and by this time we both were known on campus as sincere student athletes, contributing on the football field, but equally engaged in our academic pursuits.

John, with his argumentative, yet playful and friendly nature, would stop by our room from time to time to visit. No football players were rarely seen in the AD, or Athletic Dorm during those days. During these days, John was not known as a fan or enthusiast by the football team and student body, but as a critic of the program and Coach Cooley.

John was a statistician for both the football and basketball program along with being the Editor-in-Chief of MVSU's Student Newspaper, the Delvian Gazette. With this skill set and bulldog tenacity packed into a small frame, John's views were conceived and refined from a different end of the spectrum, in comparison to the average fan. In this regard, he offered sincere feedback concerning the football program and was often ridiculed for his views and sometimes critical assessment of the football program.

Through Facebook post, time has revealed that John Boy was and is perhaps the MVSU Football Program's Biggest Fan and Historian… John Boy has eloquently documented and celebrated most, if not all of our 1984 Teammates with not just common football facts, but intimate details concerning the personalities, hometown, values, and each of our contributions to our team, MVSU and the broader community. For these reasons, John was simply the right person to coauthor this book dedicated to the life of Coach Archie "The Gunslinger" Cooley.

As Darryl's college roommate, Best friend, and Uncle Al to his children, I am not surprised of his many accomplishments on and off the field. Darryl is one of the most tenacious and loyal people that I have met in life. But his tenacity and strength, are reflective of the MVSU Football Program of the Archie Cooley era, as a Father figure first, and a Coach second.

Coach Cooley quickly advised our freshman class of 1983 to "get your education, because I am going to get my football". Arriving from Mattie T. Blount High School in Prichard, Alabama having lost both parents during my childhood, I was instantly drawn to Coach Cooley because of his interest in my personal life circumstances and well-being first (football player second), contrary to other recruiters of that day. Coach Cooley's devotion and stewardship to excellence are perhaps best documented by the accomplishments of Jerry "World" Rice, who has rewritten many of Pro Football's records for receiving and is arguably one of the best players to have ever played the game.

What was undocumented before this book, is how Coach Cooley reshaped the lives and hearts of young men, and women, in the Mississippi Delta, who now lead in all facets of life throughout our nation, as fathers , community leaders, educators, innovators, entrepreneurs, technologist, coaches, community activist, and more importantly, Brothers to the Mississippi Delta and an important era in College Football.

To football historians, sports enthusiasts, interested readers, and fans of this era, this book documents a great chapter in the game of football, and its impact on communities across our nation. To the Valley Family, this is the work of two of our own, about one of our own, a celebration of a great past, and a compass to our shared future.

Respectfully,

Albert G. Edwards, August 29, 2019

TRAINING UP A CHILD
Growing up in the Segregated South

Archie Cooley and his siblings

Archie Lee Cooley was born in Sumrall, Mississippi, on March 18, 1939. Both of his parents were also from Sumrall. The Cooley family moved to Laurel, Mississippi, soon after his father took a job at the well-known Laurel Masonite Plant, where he would earn $85 dollars a week. Cooley's father worked hard to take care of his family. He was a smart man and very driven, one of the very few with an entrepreneurial spirit in Laurel during this period. These were trying times, and it was certainly even more risky for blacks to own businesses, but Cooley's father was determined. He was not afraid of the financial risks or racism he was going to face and tried his best at owning and operating several businesses, including a café, after which he opened a gas station and even took a run at used car sales. He had a knack for sales, and he passed that skill on to his sons.

Cooley's Father

Both Cooley boys would follow in the footsteps of their father, and with the drive and will he instilled in them to work hard; they also set out to become entrepreneurs. He told them both early on that he would provide what they needed for school and home, but they had to earn their own spending money. Albeit spent on sweet snacks, sodas, and whatever other delights they could afford, they both liked spending money without having to ask their father for it.

Cooley's father owned multiple businesses in Laurel, Mississippi

The boys put their heads together on several business ventures in the neighborhood. The most memorable says Cooley, was their scrap metal business. Yes, I kid you not; young Archie Cooley was a scrap metal salesperson. He and his brother would scour the neighborhood and collect all kinds of metal while rolling through the streets and alleyways and sell it at the local scrap metal facility. Cooley's father was a fair man, and while he did not hand out money, he showed his boys how to earn every penny they needed. Cooley laughs as he talks about it, saying, "He told us, 'You better get out there and earn what you need, because it's all you are going to get.'" Their father would never take any of their earnings from their business ideas. Cooley says this was a great lesson for him and his brother. They were being taught to work hard and earn the money they needed for the things they wanted to have.

Cooley speaks very highly of his parents. They taught him many important life lessons and encouraged him to stay focused on his education. Although he was mild mannered as a child, Cooley displayed a confident demeanor and spoke his mind. He was the oldest of his siblings, four sisters as well as his younger brother. Side by side, Cooley was the smaller of the two boys, but he had a big personality.

Cooley in younger days

While growing up in the projects in Laurel, Mississippi, during a time when segregation was prominent, Cooley and his siblings were taught to be mindful of their surroundings. They were taught to be careful about where they went and what they said, and most importantly, to be home before dark. There were a few times in Cooley's early life when he disobeyed his father's rules, but for the most part, he was never troublesome as a child or during his teenage years. His father, although a stern man, provided the right level of conversation and fear to keep him and his siblings in line and alive.

Cooley says with a voice of defense, "My father opened a service station near the Masonite plant; this was the local plant where many people in Laurel worked after graduating high school. He talks about how some of the white folks did not want him to own the service station in that popular location, so they would break out the windows and toss paint all over the building." Eventually, Cooley remembers his father giving up and moving on because of the constant threat and problems he was experiencing. These were harsh times for black business owners in Mississippi, and the Cooley's had their share of problems trying to run successful businesses in Laurel.

Cooley tells a story he remembers while in downtown Laurel, when black people wearing sunglasses was a problem and would have them taken, thrown on the ground, and stomped on by white men to keep them from looking at a white woman walking nearby.

He explained how the level of fear that black folks experienced was intense, especially when one police officer could walk into a crowd of 600 black people and say, "Shut up," and the place would be silent. He said that was the type of control they had over the black community during that time. He remembers asking his father once, "Are you afraid of them?" His father replied affectionately, "Boy, I'm trying to save your life, and if you go out there and run your mouth too much, they will hurt you, and nothing will be done about it."

Cooley learned how to adjust to this environment and did what he had to do to stay out of trouble. He remembers it was not the children being accosted in most cases. It was adults that would do things that white folks did not like and would be attacked for it. Cooley does not place much emphasis on race being a factor in his early life as far as he remembers. Even though things were happening around him, for the most part he did most things that he wanted to. In fact, he states how he was not afraid during these times but remembers how his father was.

Like all kids, Cooley had his share of scary moments. He remembers his friend Bill "Bucket" Williams had to save his life while he and two other friends were playing in a nearby river. He had already been warned by his father about playing in the river because he couldn't swim, but he went anyway. Cooley almost drowned after the branch he was swinging from broke. He fell into the rushing river, and luckily Bucket jumped in, swam near him, and saved him before he went under. The sadder side of the story is that Bucket could not get to his other friends in time to save them from tragedy.

If almost drowning was not bad enough, one summer day while riding on the back of his sister's bike, his foot was caught in the rear wheel and the spokes cut the back of his heal badly. His mother did not know what to do to stop the bleeding except bandage it. She tried to wash it down and change the bandages several times, but nothing worked to stop the bleeding. She decided to rush him to his aunt's house, who put his foot in Epsom salt and used a few other of her home remedies to save his foot. Cooley thought for sure he was going to lose his foot and possibly any chance of playing sports, but luckily, the summer months gave him time to heal and be ready for sports when school started.

Cooley's father was not much of a church going man, so he and his siblings would get their spiritual teachings from his mother's side of the family. She would always take him and his siblings to church because she wanted them to be good, well-rounded kids, although they never participated in any after church activities. Cooley's father, on the other hand, maintained family principles and had one rule that he did not play around with. He always reminded Cooley and his siblings to be in the house before dark or else he would lock them out. Cooley says, "You would have to sleep on the front porch if you didn't make it in time, and he meant it." Cooley and his siblings knew that when it came to curfew there was no room for error, so they did not challenge this rule at all.

High School, the Journey Begins

High school was the launching pad for Cooley and the beginning of his legendary sports journey. He credits his mother's side of the family for his athletic ability since his grandmother was from the Black Foot Indian Tribe. Leveraging his talent, he played football, basketball, baseball, and ran track. He remembers that if you were a certain size and body type, you were sure to be asked by a coach to play football. Your father would make you play, he said. This was the case for him in his 9th grade year at Oak Park High, where Coach Russell Frye, an Alcorn graduate and the head coach, saw him standing outside with his friends and asked why he was not at practice. "Son," he said, "you need to come out for football."

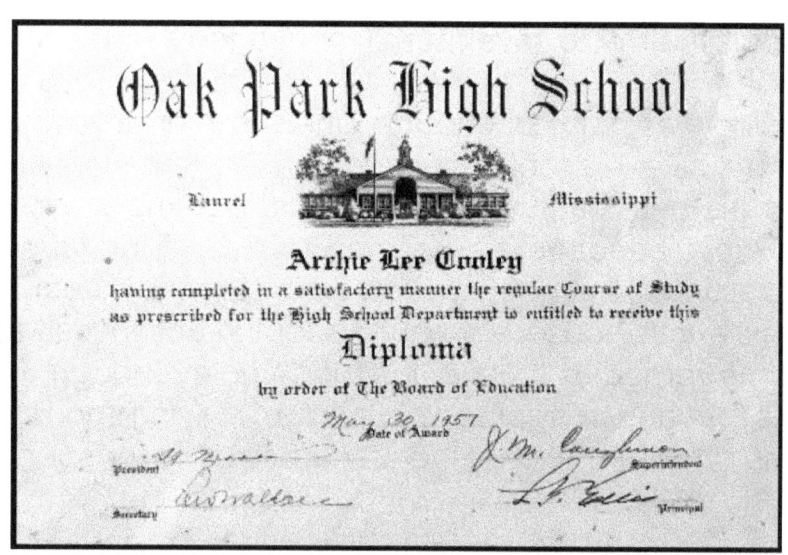

Cooley's Oak Park High diploma

Cooley was not interested in football, he wanted to be in the band, and tenor sax was his instrument of choice. Coach Frye told Cooley, "Well, I'm going to see your old man about that," and that he did. Cooley said when he got home his father told him that Coach Frye had called him. The next few words his father uttered would change Cooley's direction, and his life. He told Cooley, "You're going to play football, son, so get ready because I'm taking you to practice." Cooley said there was nothing he could say or do about it, and shortly afterwards he and his father were on their way to the field. From that day forward, Cooley and football would be inextricably tied together.

Cooley speaks fondly of Coach Russell Frye, his high school coach. He was a great inspiration for Cooley and gave him the basis for his coaching philosophy. Cooley said, "I wanted to be like Coach Frye, so I did the things that made Coach Frye successful, but on a bigger scale." He was impressed with how Coach Frye could see plays on TV and insert them into his play scheme. His philosophy, Cooley remembers, was "Work hard, and especially, out-work your opponent." Cooley adopted this philosophy so that if his opponent worked five hours, he would work six, and that was the key to his success as a player and coach. It is also worth mentioning that under Coach Frye, Cooley never lost a single football game.

As a high school football player, Cooley remembers playing against teams from Alabama and most often Mississippi teams from Waynesboro, Meridian, Lacombe, Lanier, Jackson, and Hattiesburg. He remembers the talk being that whoever won between Hattiesburg and Laurel usually won the Big Eight Championship. During his four years of high school, he never lost to Hattiesburg. Cooley was also a basketball player and the highest scorer on his team with an average of 18 points per game. He was versatile and showed many talents, and because of his commitment and desire to win, he put in whatever work was necessary. His investment paid off, as the work always returned positive results, including his selection as the Big Eight Conference Player of the Year for three of Oak Park's four winning seasons.

Although Cooley's father worked and ran businesses, his family was not rich or well off, according to Cooley. He knew that the only way he would go to college was by getting an athletic scholarship. He remembers his parents telling him to make sure he was paying attention to his schoolwork so that he could make good grades. They also stayed on top of him and talked about doing well in sports so that when the time came, he would get offers for a scholarship.

THE TIGER YEARS

Football

Cooley at Jackson State University

Big John Merritt, Jackson State University's (JSU) head football coach and another pillar in Cooley's career, sent one of his recruiters to talk to Cooley his senior year about playing football for JSU. Cooley, at the time, also had offers from other schools that were interested in his talent, including the University of Arkansas at Pine Bluff; Miles College at Fairfield, Alabama; and Lane College at Jackson, Tennessee, but Cooley admits his first love was in Louisiana, Grambling State University.

He wanted to follow his high school teammates and friends who had received scholarships to Grambling; however, legendary SWAC coach Eddie Robinson uttered words to Cooley that one day he would wish he had taken back. He told Cooley, "Son, you have the skills and the heart, but you are too small to play for me." This statement did not sit well with Cooley, who had developed a high confidence level in his ability at the time. He had never lost a high school football game and felt he was in the driver's seat, at least in deciding on which SWAC university he wanted to attend. When he realized this was not the case, it created quite a bit of animosity between the two. Later, things would end in Cooley's favor, both as a player and a coach.

Cooley was also excited about playing at JSU. He was impressed with Big John Merritt as well and told the recruiter to have Coach Merritt come and get him. Coach Merritt did not waste any time, and after receiving the message, he headed straight to the projects where Cooley lived and signed him to his football team at Jackson State. Cooley now had a chip on his shoulder and planned to make sure Eddie Robinson remembered who he was when JSU would play Grambling.

As the future unfolded, Cooley and Eddie Robinson had a few showdowns. Cooley remembers running by the Grambling bench to tell Eddie Robinson before the game, "Watch me, and see what I do since I'm too small to play for you." Cooley was on a mission and fondly remembers, after beating Grambling, Eddie would see him coming and say, "Don't tell me, don't tell me. I know, I know." Cooley said, "I tried to tell you I could play, I told you I had enough size to play on your team." Cooley said Eddie Robinson told him, "I wish I had signed you, Cooley, but it's too late to think about. Congrats on a hell of a game." That was vindicating for Cooley, and in his own fashion, he said, "Thanks, and by the way, I'm going to have a hell of a game every time I play against Grambling."

Cooley with Big John Merritt

JSU was at its peak with Big John Merritt as head coach, Joe Gilliam, another Cooley mentor, as defensive coordinator, and Alvin Coleman as offensive coordinator. Merritt allowed Gilliam and Coleman to run the team while he worked up and out activities and took care of the team. Cooley says that this staff was 10 years ahead of their time. They were great coaches. Big John took his team seriously and made sure his players were taken care of.

Cooley preparing to play against Mississippi Valley State University

In the Center of it All

Cooley turned out to be quite the star player at JSU as a running back his first year, scoring six touchdowns. Merritt told him, "We can't keep you out of the end zone. Keep it up!" After that year, JSU was not comfortable with their choice of center for the season. Cooley overheard the conversation and offered to take on the position. Since he was a backup running back and wanted more playing time, the opportunity interested him. The coaches asked him if he was sure he wanted the change, and Cooley said, "If you let me in at center, I'll be a starter." They let him change, and Cooley never looked back.

Jackson State University football team

After years of winning since his high school days, it was time for Cooley to learn the hard lesson of how to handle defeat. He lost his first game ever against Southern, and he could not contain his emotions. He teared up in the locker room and was approached by his coach, who asked what was wrong. Cooley's world was upside-down, his voice full of emotion when he said for the first time, "We just lost!" Quietly, his coach told him something he had never had to understand before, "We lose sometimes,

Cooley, it's part of the game." Cooley had such a winning spirit from his high school days that he was devastated by the loss, but more disheartening to him was that others around him were not bothered. He now understood that you win some and you lose some, but what is most important is what you learn from it, apply it to get better, and try again.

Baseball

On Sundays, Cooley would go to Yazoo City to play pickup games of baseball with his friends and brothers Herman and Wardell Leach. He was good at pitching, and during his first game in Yazoo, he pitched a shutout and was asked to join the team permanently. The JSU baseball coach happened to be at one of their games, noticed Cooley's talent, and asked him to try out for the Jackson State team. He impressed the coach during tryouts and was signed to the team immediately. Cooley was now not only a star football player, but also a star baseball player at JSU.

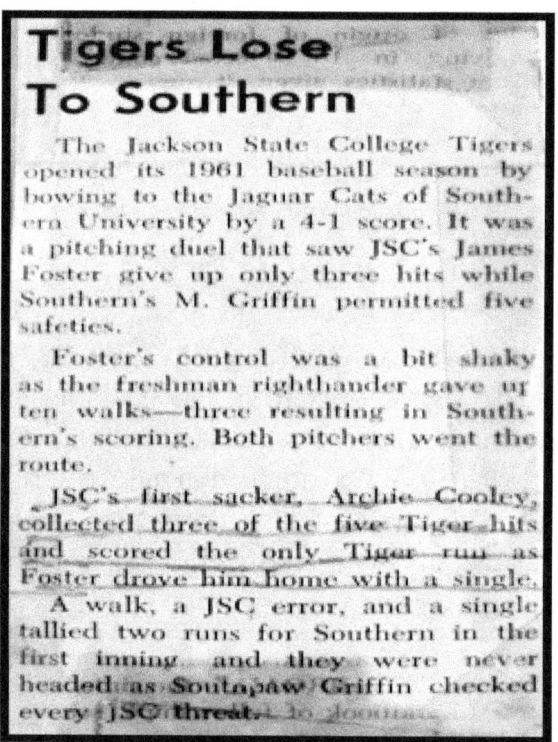

Cooley was a standout JSU baseball player

Cooley played baseball his last two years at JSU, and more than likely would have started earlier if the baseball coach had known about him. Cooley did well in baseball and earned a lettered for his efforts.

Cooley's parents were instrumental in pushing him to focus on his educational foundation, so he was a decent student and able to maintain his grades while playing sports. He was a high school honor student his junior and senior year, but despite his foundation, his first two years at JSU were typical. He did what all freshman do when they arrive at college and realize the freedom they now have. They party! And that he did.

Love at First Sight

Georgia Cooley in the JSU band

Not too far into his junior year, however, he met the love of his life, a pretty young lady with a heart of gold who slowed things down for him and made him focus. It was just what he needed at the right time. Cooley remembers the encounter as if it was yesterday. He tells about preparing to travel to Grambling for their next football game, getting on the bus and waiting to leave when he saw a tall, thin, young woman walk by. Her beauty struck him in a way no other girl had.

At the time, she was walking with her boyfriend, and Cooley asked his friend sitting next to him, "Hey, who is that pretty lady?" His friend told him that the young woman he was eyeing was Harold's girlfriend, to which Cooley replied, "Oh no, no, that will not be Harrold's girlfriend for too much longer." With certainty in his heart, he said, "I'm going to marry that young lady."

Georgia and Archie

One thing about Archie Cooley, he is a man of his word. He did marry Georgia in 1962, and he has been happily married to her for 57 years. They were blessed with two beautiful children, Dwight and Lisa Cooley.

Dwight and Lisa Cooley

Dwight, a student at Tennessee State during Cooley's Valley years, remembers visiting the campus and experiencing the excitement and change towards anticipation of a winning football team. This excitement had affected the students and the faculty, Dwight recalls. Dwight was close in age to many of the players and remembers feeling apart of the brotherhood that had developed amongst the team. He said the odds were stacked against his dad since the team wasn't winning when he arrived. They had not won many games and hadn't beaten Jackson State in 28 years. Dwight says his father's philosophy was the main factor behind his success at the Valley, to outwork your opponent. Dwight, like his father and grandfather, has followed their entrepreneurial spirit as he is also the owner of a restaurant in Dallas, Texas.

Georgia, Archie, Dwight and Lisa Cooley

Lisa remembers an awesome and exciting time. She said her father never stopped being the gunslinger. Always looking for how to get better. Even as a father, he wanted to know how he could improve her life. Always wanting to be the best at whatever he did. She remembers her 11th grade year and becoming a part of the Valley vibe living on campus, not going to school or leaving early to attend a press conference or travel with the team to a big game. This all meant she and Mrs. Cooley would need to look their best and that required shopping and beauty appointments which Lisa didn't mind obliging. It was a joyous and lively time at Mississippi Valley for Lisa. Today she herself, like her father, takes pride in being and doing her best as she is a mentor and educator.

A SEMI-PRO BASEBALL PLAYER
The Laurel Black Cats

In 1961, Cooley was recruited by the Laurel Black Cats, a Semi-Pro baseball team in Laurel, Mississippi. He would sometimes hitch a ride home from Jackson State with a classmate on Saturdays and played on Sundays. The Black Cats needed a pitcher, and Cooley fit the bill. He did well with the Black Cats and was thought to go further in the future. He recalls being on a winning team and playing against teams from Mobile, New Orleans, Meridian, Hattiesburg, Gulfport, and Biloxi. Cooley eventually ran into a problem with transportation to get him to and from the games and eventually had to give up his opportunity with the Black Cats and his future in semi-pro baseball.

A LEGEND IN THE MAKING
From Player to Coach

Cooley remembers several moments that have influenced his career, but one of his most memorable was how Coach Frye, his high school coach, would watch a football game on TV and draw up plays as he watched. He would then put them in his playbook, practice them, and was very successful when using them. This and many of his techniques were seeds that were planted into Cooley's mind that he would never forget. These seeds would lay the foundation for his future success as a coach.

Plans Interrupted

The McLaurin Attendance Center in Magee, Mississippi, is where the transition began for Cooley, moving from player to coach. He taught health and physical education while coaching football and softball. Big John Merritt, his coach at JSU, was instrumental in Cooley obtaining this first coaching opportunity, and at three thousand dollars a year, Cooley surely had to be mindful of how he spent his money. He coached at the McLaurin Attendance Center for one year, finishing with a 6-4 season. After that year, Cooley's plans for the future were halted abruptly when he was drafted into the military.

This event threw a wrinkle in things for his coaching ambitions, and he recalls the Laurel Military Draft Board manager who made the decision to draft him. It seems the manager had been angry with Cooley for getting help from Shi Ram, a wealthy grocer Cooley previously worked for during the off-season in high school. Mr. Ram spoke to the board about waving Cooley's draft decision because he was teaching school, which was part of draft regulations. With his help, Cooley was able to avoid his draft fate for one year, but the following year he again received a letter from the board and entered the U.S. Army.

SERVING HIS COUNTRY
A Military Jock

Cooley in military uniforms

Not many know that Archie Cooley was drafted into the military in 1962. He was sent to Fort Seal, Oklahoma, for basic training, then to Fort Bragg to begin his military career. As things turned out, his athletic talent did not go unnoticed in the military either. He was recruited to play football for the Army after they heard he was a football star at JSU. Next, when the baseball coach found out he also played baseball at JSU, he recruited Cooley to play baseball for the

Army as well. None of this sat well with Cooley's first sergeant, who did not like the fact that all his time was being spent on sports. He told Cooley that he could not be in his company and be a jock. Luckily for Cooley, the football coach was a colonel and the baseball coach were a major. Both outranked the first sergeant.

Cooley in uniform

They told Cooley not to worry, saying they would take care of the situation and make sure he did not have any more problems. Cooley played football and baseball while in the Army for 2 years, but he was about to run into another snag with the military.

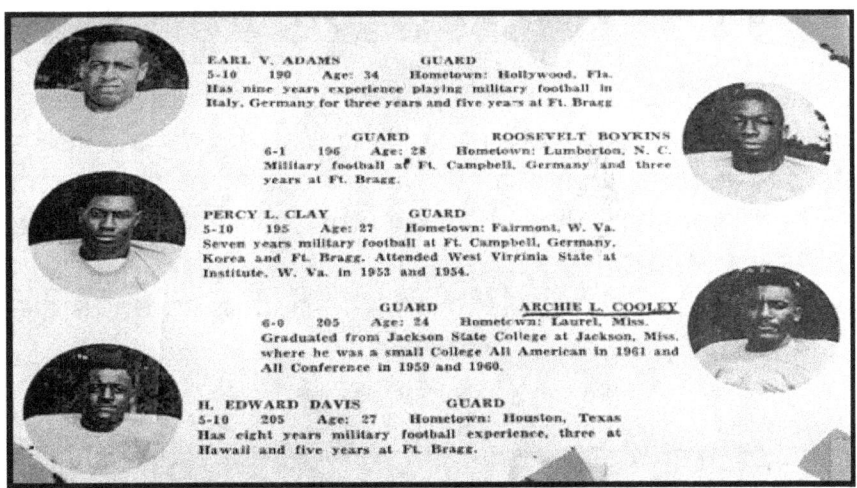

Cooley was a standout athlete while in the military

Cooley was about to be shipped off to Germany for his next assignment. Since he did not want to go off to Germany, he met with his military commanders and explained that his brother was already in Germany, and both he and his brother did not need to be over there. Because Cooley was not afraid and spoke up, he did not have to go and eventually was honorably discharged in 1964.

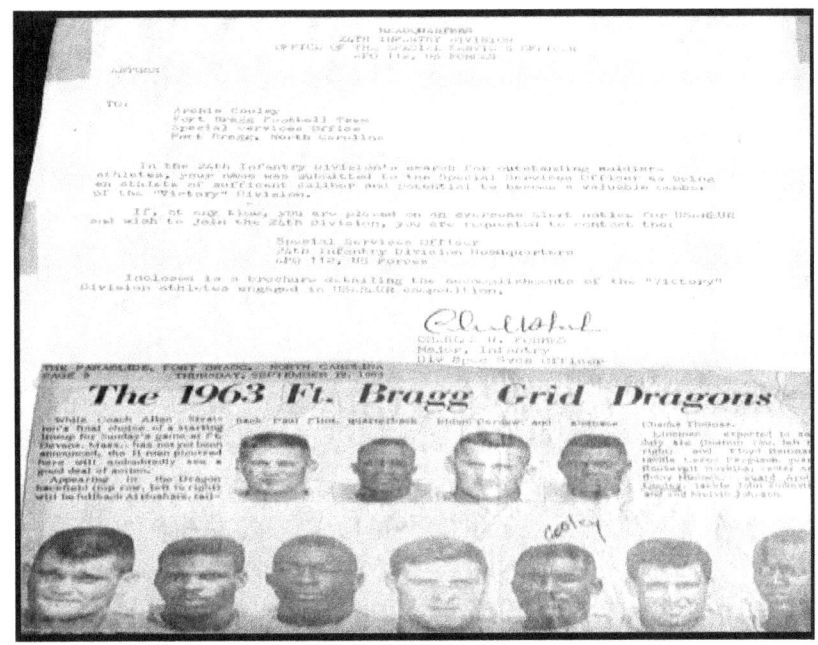

Cooley the military jock

After serving his country and returning home, Cooley was back to doing what he loved, coaching. Right out of the Army he was hired by Coach Willie C. Jones at Southside High School in Heidelberg, Mississippi. There he coached for seven years, winning several championships as a girls' basketball coach. His record reflects a 78-game winning streak, a host of regional championships, and two state championships. His strategy was to practice his girls against the 8th grade boys' team. He believed he had to have them play like the boys. He ran zones mostly, but would double-team the ball handler, forcing the ball to his opponent's weakest player.

Southside girls' basketball champions

Adding to the list of coaching greats and mentors influencing Cooley's career was Coach Marino Casem, also known as "The Godfather." He hired Cooley in 1971, who coached alongside him for two and a half years at Alcorn as a defensive coordinator. Cooley was in a winning program with Casem, adding to his repertoire the tools he would carry with him once he became a head coach. Cooley was struggling with the salary he was being paid, and for everything Casem did for him, he was grateful, but he had to look forward to bigger opportunities.

Cooley when coaching girls' basketball

His next break was not very far away, as Cooley moved to Tennessee in 1974 to earn a much higher salary and join Big John Merritt and Coach Joe Gillam, two of his favorite mentors and coaches while he was a player at JSU. Cooley accepted a position coaching the defensive line and primarily the Bear team, running offensive plays against Tennessee State's starting defense. Gillam, the defensive coordinator, gave Cooley the opportunity to test and polish his play design skills, push the envelope, and challenge the norms of football strategy. Cooley loved every minute of it. He was stacking up his favorite plays and cataloging them in his playbook, including the very one he would use in the future to establish his legacy.

Tennessee State University coaching staff

Cooley says he was having a great deal of fun in his early career, but he was limited due to most of his experience being on the offensive side of the ball. Later, when he became a head coach, not knowing much about coaching defense was an enormous challenge. On top of all that pressure he was out there by himself; he had no assistant coaches, so he had to reach back for help.

That assistance came in the name of Joe Gillam, with whom he had built a solid relationship. Cooley says Coach Gilliam was pleased to know that Cooley wanted his assistance, and he was more than happy to help him. Gillam talked him through this period, explaining what he needed to do and how to get it done. Ever studying the game, Cooley got better and better at coaching his defense.

THE VALLEY YEARS

Cooley ready for the challenge as head coach

When Mississippi Valley President Dr. Earnest A. Boykin was searching for a head coach, two names were presented to him: James T. Thomas from Old

Miss and Archie Cooley from Tennessee State. The board's decision was to go with Thomas, but after the first year the team revolted and went on a strike. In response, Dr. Boykin wasted no time in contacting Cooley. He had wanted to hire Cooley initially but had been out voted by the board. Cooley was elated to receive the call, as this was the head coaching opportunity he had been looking for. His dreams were coming to fruition!

Cooley remembers attending a football program shortly thereafter in Greenwood, Mississippi, where Lou Holtz was featured as a guest. Cooley took the opportunity to speak with Lou and asked him for advice as a first-time head coach. Lou was gracious with his wisdom and said, "The best advice I can give you, Cooley, is don't fight the media. Agree with them when you are wrong and work with them. Be nice, and you'll be fine." Cooley thought that would be easy and replied, "I like to talk, and I'll make sure to take care of them. My door will always be open."

It was spring of 1980 when Cooley first set foot on the campus of Mississippi Valley State University. He was about to etch into everyone's memory the journey of a great football team and their magical season, a season that remains a topic of sports conversation and recognition to this day some thirty years later.

As best as he could, Cooley assembled a coaching and training staff on a shoestring budget. He recruited players with big hearts and a desire to help him bring his coaching vision to life.

Cooley continues the journey through Mississippi

Featuring Hall of Fame wide receiver, Jerry "World" Rice, quarterback Willie "Satellite" Totten, and a host of unsung players that made it through Cooley's rigorous training camps, practice, and enduring football program. Amongst themselves, they were known as the "Red Devils," a title of endearment teammates did not assume but earned through sheer will, sweat, and focus on Cooley's every word.

Willie "Satellite" Totten and Jerry "World" Rice

These players were mere boys as they arrived at the Valley, but after their journey through the many trials and challenges Cooley would put them through, they were young men proud of their Red Devil badge of honor.

Through Cooley's program, they became a band of brothers who are a close-knit group even today. That bond still brings them together as they arrive at Valley for homecoming, just as they did for training camp, year after year. They check-in, sharing hugs and handshakes of pride and joy to see each other. Many of them are now fathers, passing on the lessons learned while under Cooley's tutelage; businessmen and managers who gained a great understanding of strategy, hard work, and diligence; authors who write with passion and truth; educators and counselors who share their learning and experiences to uplift others; philanthropists who give because they were provided with opportunities through football; and yes, coaches, who are passing on what they learned from Cooley and his legendary football program.

A Recruiting Genius

Cooley has an eye for talent

Cooley was looking to make his mark as head coach of a little-known school in the Mississippi Delta. Little did he know he was on a path to awaken the sports world, set new records, and leave tracks in history to be talked about for decades. With a recruiting budget of less than four thousand dollars, he began his work already behind the curve. Archie Cooley had a plan, and along with a wealth of experience he gained all the way back from Oak Park High through Jackson, the Army, the trails of Tennessee, and back down to Mississippi, he still had an uphill battle ahead of him. All Cooley was missing was a team, a group of committed men willing to trust him and his program.

The genius behind Cooley's recruiting strategy included something incredibly simple, but at its best held the key to getting him the players he needed to fulfill his grand plan with a miniscule budget. He received 20 cents a mile and $13 a day for his meals, but he did something that coaches from major universities in Alabama, Mississippi, and Louisiana did not. He went into the homes of his recruits. From his own experience and observations, Cooley understood that when it came time to decide which school to sign with, it was not the fathers of the players he was looking for who were the determining factor, it was the mothers. The mothers had the final say on where these players would go. He could talk to the fathers until he was blue in the face all the way up to signing day, but it was the mothers whose conversations determined what was best for their sons.

Cooley knew that on his shoestring budget he had to get straight to the point. That meant visiting and convincing each mother that MVSU was the optimum school for her son's talents and aspirations. He knew that included, if offered, eating her dinner. He understood this was her way of finding out who she was possibly sending her son off with and if Cooley could be trusted. Even further, Cooley knew this dinner, this rite of passage, must be spoken of in good terms, even if the food was not good. This was his best opportunity to have a convincing conversation, and like an artist, Cooley managed to paint success in the future of each of his recruits. He recruited players from the east and west coasts, north and south on a shoestring budget, and in doing so he was able to masterfully build the foundation for his dream team.

Cooley wins his first collegiate game, MVSU vs Morris Brown

The Architect of the Spread and No Huddle Offense

Over his coaching career, Cooley became a play-making architect like his mentor back in high school, Coach Frye. He developed an offense that would be studied by coaching teams nation-wide, particularly because it was a system that went far beyond the norm.

Cooley calls plays from the sideline with his no huddle offense

Some said it was too gimmicky, but it got the attention of not only other NCAA schools, but also NFL teams who began adding similar plays to their programs. Some say the West Coast offense started at Mississippi Valley and was Cooley's initial design. In short, Cooley was doing what most were afraid to try, stretching the offense and daring defensive coordinators to line up against his adjustable strategy. He wanted to win, and he would do it with the hand he was dealt. He found himself at a small school in a small town with a small budget. Along with that, however, he had a big dream and a playbook that would help make it a reality. His plan would bring about a lasting historical relevance to the State of Mississippi, Itta Bena, and Mississippi Valley State University.

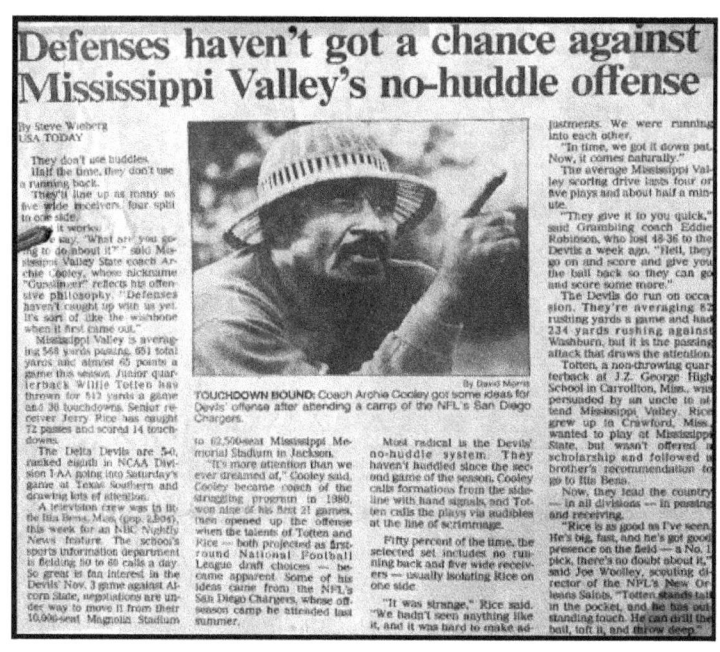

Cooley's no huddle offense

Cooley had designed an innovative passing offense that included no huddle, five wide receivers, no backs, and four receivers on one side, all of which were reconfigurable from the sideline. This offense was the catalyst for Cooley becoming the winningest coach in the history of Mississippi Valley State football.

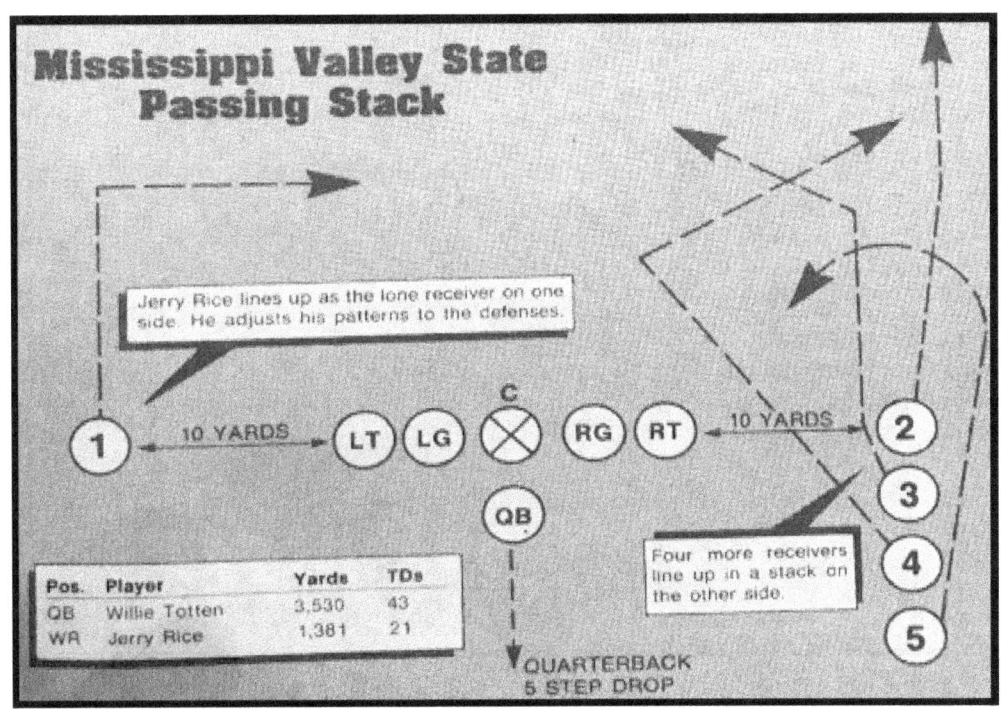

Cooley's Stack Offense

He developed the offense from plays he assembled when he ran the Tennessee State scout team. He had also saved for his book the best plays that the opponent ran against Tennessee State's defense, back when Coach (Joe) Gilliam was the defensive coordinator. Cooley said, "I could hardly wait to run my plays during practice." It was the highlight of the day for him, and because he took pride in looking for defensive weaknesses and bolstering the strength of his plays, his skills in offensive play design grew better and better. These plays became the basis for an explosive offense that opened the opportunity to run the ball more effectively when needed.

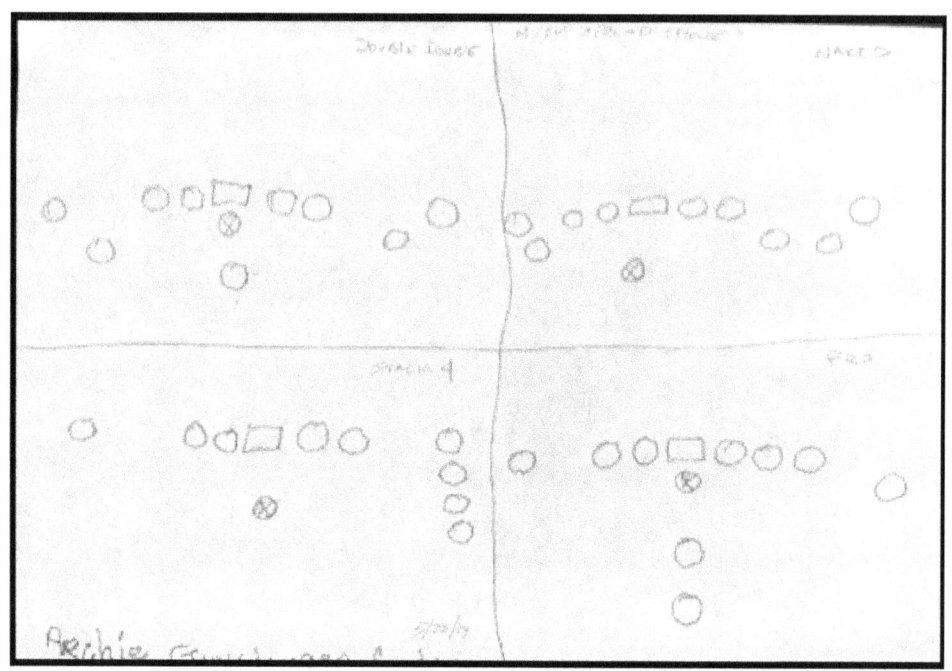

Cooley's hand drawn Run and Gun Offense

The 1983 season gave Cooley his first taste of success. He was determined to transform his offense into an unrelenting touchdown-scoring machine, and with the 1984 training camp beginning, he had a playbook of over 200 plays that utilized just about every imaginable formation to confuse opponents. He would make calls from the sideline, triple-stack, slot, and one back to adjust his lineups. He would sometimes use the traditional formations and pass or run just to confuse the defense.

Gunslinger unleashing his high-powered offense

He would often put on his architect hat and add a new wrinkle to his scheme. He would ask his coaching staff for feedback, especially when he planned to try something completely out of the ordinary. On one occasion, he asked what they thought about running a no huddle offense, not only as a 2-minute drill situation but for the whole game. He would make all his calls from the sideline as he had done before. No other team in college or pros would ever think to do this the whole game. It was another genius masterpiece, a nuclear option on the gridiron.

Cooley was energized and immediately began putting his plan into motion. This idea was destined to be his signature strategy, and soon he would be recognized for its significant impact on offenses across the nation.

Training Camp

Every fall, Cooley's football players were the first to arrive on campus, many weeks before the rest of the student body. They came in groups with trailers hitched to the back of their cars and trunks stuffed with everything they owned. Freshmen players would roll in looking bewildered, trying to figure out where they would be housed and with whom they would share a room. This was an important orientation as well as a lifelong moment, because whomever this person was, they would become "roomies," and that term would link them to one another forever. The upperclassmen, now part of the Red Devil posse, would show up gleeful and happy to see their roomie and Red Devil brethren. A few days of this lighthearted interaction would take place, but in the back of everyone's' mind was what lay ahead. Freshmen had no idea what they were about to experience; the first step in Cooley's training camp.

The Cooley challenge was set. In order to get your equipment, you had to endure his god-awful two weeks of three-times-a-day, track meet-style conditioning program, which included dividing up into groups of each position. Offense and defense ran in separate heats of 220 relays, quarter miles, and a final one-mile run, all timed to push players to the brink of their limits. Throughout those fourteen days, many just plain quit and never even saw the football equipment they had hoped to wear with pride. At 5:30 a.m., players were wakened to loud whistles blaring throughout the athletic dorm. The welcome bliss of sleep was interrupted by conscious awareness of aches, pain, and soreness from the days before, and all of it foreshadowed the physical and emotional demands of the day ahead. The heat exhaustion, vomiting, and cramps all were Cooley's way of driving out the quitters early on and it worked like a charm. At 11:00 p.m., you could hear noises in the hallway. They were the sounds of players who were quitting, who had given up on their quest to become Red Devils.

They were dragging their belongings down the stairs in trunks, sneaking out and across highway 82 to catch a bus ride back home while everyone else was asleep. During roll call the next morning, if a player left in the middle of the night, when his name was called a coach would yell out, "He's gone, Coach!" It would echo loud and long, as other players would then yell out the same thing. If you survived this training, you were halfway through becoming a member of the Red Devils, the brotherhood of Mississippi Valley State football players.

Practice in the "Hideaway"

Cooley on his way to the infamous Hideawa

Everyone who survived the conditioning program received their equipment and was ready to go for the first week of full gear practice, Training Camp. In the dark of morning, you could set your watch to the sound of blaring whistles and voices screaming like drill sergeants hollering at new military cadets in boot camp. Most players would try to get a precious few more minutes of napping, and then like firefighters responding to an alarm, rush to get equipment on.

Hurrying across campus to the infamous practice field, players fought swarms of mosquitoes that tracked body heat while crossing grounds laden with heavy dew. The field was tucked in the far east corner of the campus and nicknamed the "Hideaway" because it was hidden behind a row of large trees. In the summer, the Hideaway was hard, cracked, and dusty, but in the spring and winter, it was either soggy or downright muddy. Nearby was the swath of land players feared most and formally referred to as the Bean Field.

This dreaded field was long and wide, and coaches used the miles of soybean rows to punish transgressors of any commands during practice. Rolling and tumbling head over feet in the dirt for as long as it took, players would pay for their offenses until the coach would grow tired of the punishment. By the time, they arrived at the Hideaway in the morning, the players socks were bloody from the mosquitoes swatted during the cross-campus hike. The only relief was to keep moving, warming up while praying for the sun to show its face soon, which was the only antidote to the persistent swarms.

Cooley had his playbook and a wealth of coaching experience. He had a strategy for recruiting and a university behind him that needed his leadership. He had only one problem, his innovative offensive designs would take a toll on his players on offense and defense. They would need to be in ideal condition to handle the grueling practices and game time to execute his schemes with success. There would be almost no time to regroup, draw-up adjustments, or talk on the sideline. Players would have to get off their feet and on the bench as fast as they could. This was especially true for the defense because the offense, at times, could score consistently in two or three plays. Faced with that reality, Cooley upped the gain on conditioning in order to ensure the optimal shape of both offensive and defensive players and the team's readiness for the grueling task ahead.

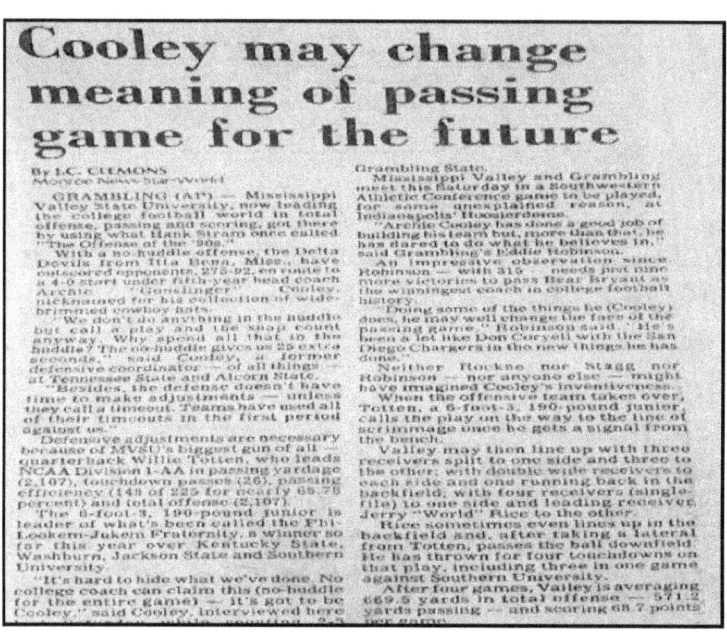

Cooley would change the game of football

Cooley practiced his two-minute drill up and down the field in the hideaway. He had plans to run this type of offense the entire game, so he had to practice it before running it during game time. The defense would have to do its best to stop it. Both offense and defense went at it with everything they had, twice and sometimes three times a day. Many would tire out, some threw up, and others would just plain quit, but this is what Cooley had convinced his players they needed to do in order to be winners. He had all the parts he needed and was building a "Red and Green Machine," a machine that would demand the nation's attention.

Rice and Totten headlining

Practice started with dreaded gassers, part of Cooley's solution to increase endurance. We started and ended practice with gassers. We all believed there was some sinister motive behind this most atrocious exercise. It seemed as if the coaches enjoyed pushing us until we gasped for air and struggle to finish. Offense and defense ran full speed from one side of the field to the other; back and forth, at a time relative to your position. If everyone made it, you were done, and if anyone did not make it everyone started over. It was another step in Cooley's plan to build a dream team, his team, Valley's most favored team. After gassers, the team rolled right into practice, offense on one end and defense on the other. Cooley's philosophy behind gassers was to train players to focus even when they are tired. He prepared his players to be ready to play four quarters of football at 100%, and his practices were based on three phases of training on technique and execution. It began with individual position training, which lead into group training, offense and defense, and finally bringing it all together with offense against defense. The last phase was Cooley's favorite, offense against defense. He was in his element, and you could see it on his face. He was eager to crank up the high-powered scoring machine he had engineered and watch it execute.

Just like his days at Tennessee State, when he took pleasure in running the scout team to try to fool the defense, he was like a kid at Christmas who just opened his brand new hot rod remote control car, loaded the batteries, and drove it across the living room floor smiling the whole time. He knew he had something special, and he could not wait to try it out in the arena while he watched everyone express their excitement and awe over the team he had put together with a minuscule budget.

"TONs of FUN"

Michael Dean, Lorenzo Clark, Christopher Haynes, Harvey Carter, James Thompson, Alvin Calhoun, Not in the picture: Joe Bridges

This offense was Cooley's pride and joy. The offensive line deemed by Cooley the "Tons of Fun" were the front linemen whose weight totaled more than a ton. Cooley had two front lines and he would swap them out individually or, in most cases, he would swap out the entire line. They were just that good. These guys were the nucleus of this high-powered Satellite Express offense.

They protected their leader, starting quarterback Willie "Satellite" Totten, a tall, long armed, large handed player Cooley recruited as a punter but turned into a quarterback. Cooley talked about his first meeting with Totten, shaking his hand and seeing that his own hand was completely covered. His mind started churning the moment that happened, and Cooley thought, "I wonder if he can throw the ball?" Shortly thereafter, the proof came, and he was not disappointed.

Totten also unveiled a cool, calm attitude with a twist a charisma like Cooley. You could tell they were completely in sync, they trusted each other. Cooley taught Totten to command his offence, use his weapons and Totten was a fast learner, and it showed, he was the player leader of the team.

Cooley's running back core was headed up by Carl "Truck" Byrum and Freddie "Fast Freddie" Parker. They were bruiser backs. They protected satellite during the passing game but when it can time to pick up ground mileage, these two managed to bull doze and pave the way towards touchdown after touchdown. They were accompanied by leaders Wilbur Corley, Walter Cox, Jeramiah "Bull" Snowden, and a young scatback Terry Coleman along with a host of other backs. Cooley continued to recruit, and he stacked the deck.

Cooley had managed to recruit a group of wide receivers who were like stallions waiting to be let out the gate. They were quick, smart, some short and some tall, but all were aggressive and did not mind mixing it up with defenders or sharing their playing time with each other. Within the ranks of leaders were Joe "Tweedy Bird" Thomas, Curtis "Bot" Debardlebon, Tony Baker, Cleo Armstrong, Maurice Wade, Willie Ware, Rodney "Thrill Hill", Dante Whitaker and Louis Watson, who also floated as a flex back.

They along with a host of other receivers were admirably known as "Phi Lookum Jukum," and they gave Cooley an advantage in creating mismatches with opposing defensive backs. This fraternity of receivers practiced the way they played, at a 100%. They were also a playful group and poked fun at each other, at the defense, and hell, they even poked fun at the coaching staff. They never worried about getting in trouble because they were "Cooley's boys." He protected them as if they were his own and they knew it. However, when they stepped onto the field, it was all about business, and they took pride in making sure they looked good and did exactly what Cooley asked them to do. They even celebrated as a group after scoring, which they did quite often.

Cooley went to visit B. L. Moor High School in Starkville, Mississippi to scout their team and while watching the game, he noticed a kid that could play multiple positions. He was intrigued by this and had his recruiting coach go see about this kid. He wanted to know more about this kid who could play multiple positions on the field. That kid turned out to be nonother than Jerry Rice. Ever the genius recruiter, Cooley went into action and drove back to Starkville to meet Rice's mother, and they hit it off. Cooley went to her home and ate her dinner and talked about his plan for Jerry after which she said, "My son is going to Valley, Coach Cooley, because I believe you will take care of him."

Jerry "World" Rice

Cooley's receivers now had their leader and little did they know he would be the future Hall of Famer, Jerry "World" Rice. Jerry set the tone and pace for the receivers during practice. He was tall, strong and fast. He earned the nicknamed World because he had large hands and could catch anything in the world. He was a quiet giant and diligent when it came to his performance. His work ethic was obvious as he practiced, because he was serious about working hard and being prepared for battle. He ran every route and blocking assignment as if he was in game situation, and he was at practice early and often stayed afterward to work on his technique. There was no doubt that Jerry was destined for greatness. He took pride in what he was doing.

Cooley would banter and challenge Coach Thomas, the defensive coordinator, during practice. He would yell from the other end of the Hideaway, "Coach Thomas, you ready down there? You know Jerry Rice can catch a BB in the dark!" This was his way of saying let's get it on, offense against defense, and he eagerly awaited this last phase every practice. It was the time to witness his machine at work, and watch Jerry do his thing!

Cooley's coaches, James Norwood, Willie Fulton, Richard West, Jonnie Thomas, Ricky Carson

Coach Cooley managed to recruit a stellar staff of coaches, including defensive coordinator Johnny Thomas and assistant coaches who drove the machine for him. We called all of them by last name, coaches Norwood, Fulton, West, and

Carson. Sometimes, depending on his mood, and you had to make sure you really felt he was in a good mood, you could call Coach Thomas, Coach "T," but only a few could call him by his real nickname, "Ripsaw!" Now just imagine why or how a coach would get a nickname like that and you will understand why it is important to know what to say to him before you approach. Just saying!

Coach Thomas readying for battle

Coach Thomas was a former linebacker at Alcorn State. He was a scholar as well as an All-American. He was a doctoral candidate and defensive genius. As defensive coordinator, Coach Thomas was just as excited about the last phase of practice, offense against defense, as Cooley was. He believed in studying your opponent, practice, and being prepared for anything. There were numerous rumors floating around about how intense he was as a player; rumors like how he completed a game playing through the pain of a broken arm.

That tenacity is what he emphasized to stop Cooley's offensive schemes, challenging his defense to play with intensity and his captain to turn up the gain. His philosophy was not just for his captain to learn his positions, but to make sure it was understood who was supporting and how on each play. He wanted his captains to think like coaches and expect performance like a coach would from each player. Roderick "Killa" Miller was in charge, but Tyrone "Stiffy" Jones, Loyd Mumphrey, Robert "Pink Panther" Sanders, Rickey "Hyperactive"

Tobin, Vincent "Undertaker" Brown, Willie "Cambodia" Branch, Darryl "Mac" McKnight and Dwayne "DT" Thomas rounded off his core of leaders.

They were expected to make damn sure everyone was around the ball at the end of every play. Any deviation was one of those things, amongst several, that would drive Coach Thomas absolutely crazy, and you did NOT want to be the cause of that. If you were, it was a sure-fire way to earn your entry into the dreaded Bean Field. If you were not hustling to the ball, everyone at practice, including Cooley, would watch you get berated by Coach Thomas all the way to the Bean Field to begin your punishment.

He would leave you there as if you did not exist and come back to practice while you were tumbling back and forth up and down the rows. Eventually he would end your punishment, but by then you were so covered in either mud or dust that most of the players felt sorry for you as a teammate. It was an eye-opening, frightening experience, especially for freshman players. At times, Cooley would intervene, yelling aloud, "Coach Thomas, that's enough! Do not kill'em down there!"

Coach Johnny "Ripsaw" Thomas getting the defense ready for battle

Coach Thomas liked the hard-hitting contact drills and practice scrimmages. Infamous for his Head Butting and Circle Up drills, he wanted to prepare players for the hard contact experienced during games. He would match defensive backs with linebackers and linebackers with lineman so there was no cheating during these drills. He was so excited about practice; he was the first to arrive and the last to leave. Sometimes, we would approach the Hideaway and notice someone laying in the middle of the field in a sweat suit, with their hood on.

It would be Coach Thomas, sprawled out in the middle of the field. Once, as we all gathered, he heard us coming, stood up, and with his hands open wide to the sun shouted, "Energize me!" At this point, we were all bewildered and worried at the same time, playfully worried. We all started saying the same thing anytime we made a good play or tackle, and it became a term of endearment for the defense.

Valley's Defense

Offense and defense scrimmage would highlight the team's strengths and weaknesses for coaches Cooley and Thomas. It was a knockdown, drag-out, full speed, bring-it-all-to-the-table round between beasts. At first, Cooley's offense had their way with the defense, scoring at will, and sometimes Cooley would throw in a wrinkle Coach Thomas had not prepared for.

In the beginning, Coach Thomas was visibly frustrated and struggled to defend the Satellite Express offense, but Cooley didn't realize his pupil was just as strategic as he was. Coach Thomas went to the drawing board, taking the defense with him and soon the defense began to turn things around. Coach Thomas had designed a defensive strategy that would stop Cooley's offense, even with Jerry Rice. No one had realized it but, all of the practice against Cooley's offense, had made the defense a much better squad. The defense had learned how to play as a complete team, backing each other up and closing running gaps and passing lanes quickly along with everyone hustling to the ball.

Now with Coach Thomas's strategy to stop the offense they were powerful. After practicing that day, the defense left the hideaway on cloud nine. They had just stopped the offense from scoring. The excitement on coach Thomas's face was something to see, it was as if he had won the lottery. His strategy had worked, his defense was solid, and his confidence was high.

This last phase became a highly competitive part of practice for every player on offense and defense. You could feel pride slowly developing throughout each side; so much so, that everyone on the field had grown eager for the scrimmage phase of practice. Cooley was a genius. He had developed a program that not only prepared players for the game, but also drove a high sense of pride and determination in each player. Confidence and strong comradery began to permeate throughout practice, as each play was executed with fiery passion on both sides of the ball.

Cooley believed in practice no matter what the circumstances were, so on the days when it rained the team would practice in the gym. Even there, it was full contact at ¾ speed. When the team needed to practice late, Cooley would move to the stadium parking lot under the lights. Again, he called for full contact and ¾ speed. There was no such thing as not practicing or days off. It was not even enough that Cooley had two practices, one in the morning and one in the afternoon.

No, not Cooley! He added another practice in the middle of the day for quarterbacks, receivers, defensive backs, and linebackers. Yes, he added 7 on 7 at high noon in the Hideaway. There is no breeze during summer in the Mississippi Delta, especially at the hottest hour of the day, but that did not matter to Cooley. He was on a mission, and that focus called for a third practice.

So, we mounted up and headed to the hideaway for a high noon shootout. This added work pushed the players to their limits and tested their desire to be Red Devils.

Cooley's secret weapon "Willie Ware"

Cooley had several secret weapons on both offense and defense, but there was one more weapon up his sleeve NCAA records had to recon with, He was nonother than Willie Ware, a small receiver with fast feet, no fear, and an eye for finding return lanes. Willie set the bar low for the return team, he only needed a small opening on both punt and kick-off returns.

With the expectation of scoring at least once per game, he weaved his way through each level of the opponent's special teams and past the kicker on his way to a touchdown.

He had everyone on both sidelines at attention, everyone in the stands prepared to stop whatever they were doing, eating a hot dog, taking a drink, going to the rest room, talking to the person next to them, stop to watch him light up the field. And he didn't disappoint. Cooley had done it again; he had recruited another standout. When he signed Willie Ware, Cooley had recruited a super star.

Cooley's Coach of the Year Awards

"Bring it up!" Those are the words Cooley would shout at the end of practice, as players would head toward him for the usual "go eat and rest, because the next practice will start before you know it" warning. You could see the look of satisfaction on both his and Coach Thomas' face as if they had accomplished a major task. They had just put the team through another gauntlet practice.

After finishing practice, it was that dreaded time again for gassers. You could see lineman slowly walking toward the sideline as if they were walking the plank, heading to a miserable ending, and it was. While all other positions hurriedly ran from side to side, the lineman strolled like a herd, kicking up dust as they gave their all to make it through the last gasser. The faster you got through gassers, the quicker you could get to the cafeteria to devour whatever food was served that day, and the players did not care what it was. After the evening meal, it was time to head down to the Devils Den to watch game films and walk through plays. These sessions usually lasted until 11:00 pm.

Players were always grateful to see Mrs. Cooley who treated the team as if they were her sons. She understood everything the players were going through and took it upon herself to provide sandwiches for all to take back to their rooms for a late-night snack. I do not think she realized how much the team looked forward to getting those sandwiches from her, especially since there was no place close to Valley to get food and no vending machines in our dorms.

Mrs. Cooley

By the time players finished evening activities it was past curfew, and the nearest store with food was Scott-Tane, a convenience store in Itta Bena some three miles away. Mrs. Cooley was always a welcome sight.

A Nation in Awe

In order to understand the 1984 season, you must go back to the year 1980. In the fall of that year, the football fortunes of the Delta Devils were not what the alumni and administration had hoped for. Coach James T Thomas was relieved of his head coaching duties after that season. The university began a nation-wide search for his replacement, and in the spring of 1981, during a news conference held on campus, Archie Cooley, Jr. was introduced.

Cooley has arrived

The Southwestern Athletic Conference (SWAC) is famous for being one of the premier conferences in black sports, and in American collegiate sports competition, period. During the 1980s, it produced some of the greatest athletes in history.

Mississippi Valley State University was not considered one of the powers in the conference. Grambling, Jackson State, and Southern were running roughshod throughout the SWAC, leaving the other conference members in the dust. All that was about to change, if Archie Cooley had something to say about it.

In his very first press conference as Valley head coach, he put the public and fellow conference members on notice that Valley's time had come. He said it was a new day for Valley football! He would go on to tell the school's administration, as well as the Valley faithful, that if they would give him time, he would "have them a football team they'd be proud of." Time was to be his friend. Thus, began the Cooley Era, amid great hype and promises of glory.

The first two seasons of Cooley's tenure were obviously seasons of rebuilding; out with the old and in with the new. There were players from the previous regime that had to be considered before anything else, and by the time the campaign of '83 rolled around, the time had come for Coach Cooley to put his plan in motion. He had assembled around him one of the greatest coaching staffs to coach SWAC football, anchored by the formidable and intensely loyal Johnny "Ripsaw" Thomas.

The Satellite Express featuring Willie "Satellite" Totten

The team's fortunes were not only set to bring overdue glory to Valley but would finally unite and bring together the whole Valley Nation. Coach Cooley would wittingly usher in "The Era of Good Feeling" at the university. Never had there been such a powerful sense of unity and spirit of cooperation as was the case during that time, all thanks to Coach Cooley and his warriors.

Defensive Captain Roderick "Killa" Miller #91

The 1983 season was the turning point toward all the great things to come. That season, the Delta Devils first set the black football world buzzing with its open-air style of playing. Coach Cooley was utilizing every weapon in his arsenal, and doing it with pinpoint accuracy, too.

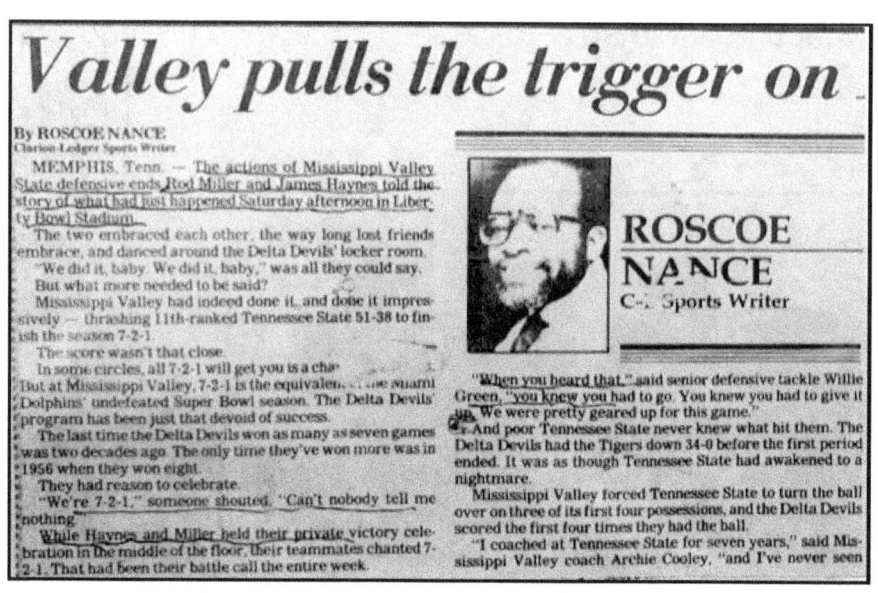

Mississippi Valley's 1983 Season was a wakeup call to the nation

That Magical 1984 Season

By John M Branson III

When the fall of 1984 arrived, it signaled the start of a great journey. The first stop on the schedule was a visit to the Kentucky State Thoroughbreds in Frankfurt, Kentucky. The Delta Devils were getting their first test, and the Devils' bus pulled out of Frankfurt with an overwhelming 86-0 triumph. The wire services started buzzing, and the other SWAC schools sat up and took notice.

A visit to Kansas was next up on the agenda. If the Devils were expecting a tough fight, they certainly did not get it. The Devils crushed the Ichabod's, leaving Topeka with a 77-15 blitzing! They also left behind a very irate Ichabod head coach who, to no avail, complained loud and long to the media about the Devils deliberately running up the score.

In Mississippi's capital city, the Devils called on the Tigers of Jackson State. After almost 30 years of futility, the Devils felt the time had come to force the bragging Tigers to show some respect. Valley Nation was more than ready, and before 52,321 trash-talking fans at Mississippi Veteran Memorial Stadium in Jackson, the drought ended as the Devils turned back the Tigers, 49-32.

Vincent Brown, Darryl Gaines, Rickey Tobin and Tyrone Jones tackle Carl Blue

To say it felt good seeing Tiger fans making their way toward the exits as the third quarter ended would be a gross understatement. The comeuppance was real!

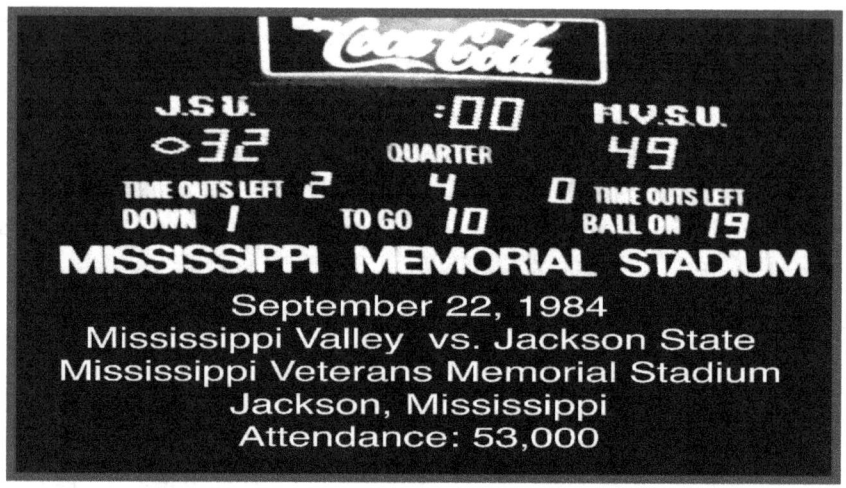

The final score and beginning of a new era for The Valley

Now sporting a perfect 3-0 record, it was time to travel to 'never friendly' Baton Rouge, Louisiana. The Jaguars of Southern University, who had narrowly escaped with a win the previous season in Itta Bena, looked to repeat. It was not to be. In an air assault for the ages, that night saw over 100 points scored. When the dust settled, the Devils marched away with a hard fought 63-45 victory.

Game three: Valley Defeats Southern

The Devils then began preparations for the team's upcoming appearance in the inaugural Circle City Classic at Indianapolis, Indiana, at the RCA Dome.

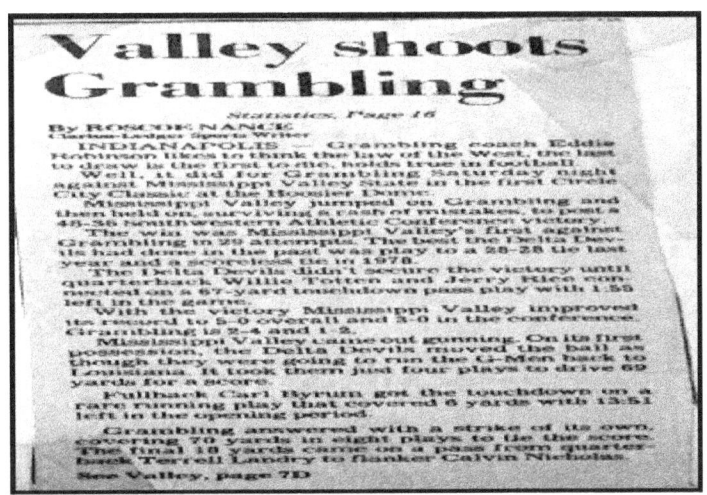

Valley wins first inaugural Circle City Classic

The challenger would be none other than Mr. Black College Football himself, Grambling State's legendary Eddie Robinson, and his always-tough Tiger squad. In front of more than 50,000 fans and a regional TV audience, the Devils humbled Coach Robinson and his Tigers, 48-36.

Arriving at the RCA Dome flanked by equipment manager Roy Hutchins

With this win, the Devils advanced to 5-0 and reached the apex in the Sheridan Poll - #1; a spot they would occupy for the next three weeks. They had by now become the most written about black football team of the last half century! The eyes of the national sports world were focused solely on the unstoppable Delta Devils and their brash talking head coach, a man who was not only talking the talk but walking the walk as well.

Valley's air assault making headlines

The nation watched in awe as Cooley marched and mowed down one opponent after the other, seemingly at will, with his unorthodox offensive scoring machine and the impenetrable Tons of Fun offensive wall out front giving protection to the Valley signal caller. Sports Illustrated and many other national publications were now beginning to make their way to sleepy little Itta Bena, seeking Cooley out, he had an offense and a defense to talk about, his Red Devil pose, he had a coaching staff and trainers to give credit to and he had a fan base that was unbelievable and he had much to say about all of them.

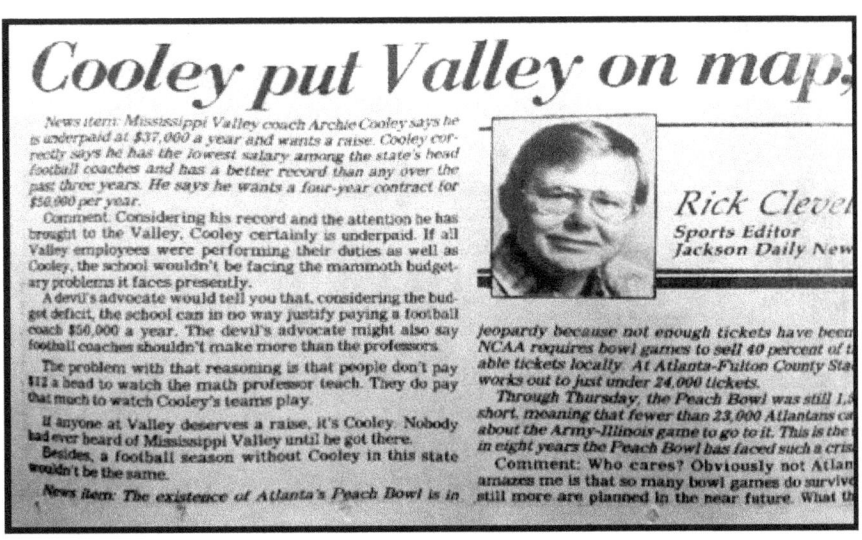

Cooley's magic is working

Houston, Texas was next up in Valley's travel plans, where another set of Tigers were waiting. The Devils were more than prepared, but the Texas Southern Tigers had no intention of going down without a fight.

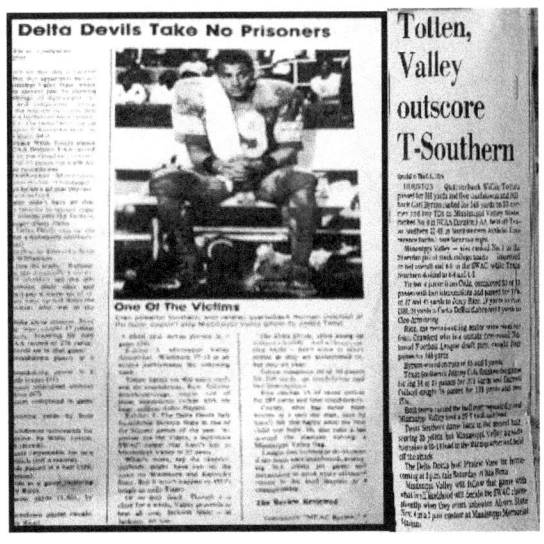

Valley wins in Texas

It was to be an offensive shootout. In the end, the Devils emerged a 55-42 victor and now stood at 6-0 overall. At this juncture, the Delta Devils had the nation's full attention. Every type of media outlet in America, it seemed, was clambering to write about Mississippi Valley State.

Cooley's air attack is on the rise

The 1984 homecoming contest would also go down as a victory. The SWAC Panthers of Prairie View A&M University visited Itta Bena on the wrong day, and Valley Nation turned out in full force to witness the devastation. The Panthers were beaten, 71-6, before a full Magnolia Stadium, enabling the Devils to sport a 7-0 record.

The "Game of the Century"

Meanwhile around the SWAC, head Brave at Alcorn State University, Marino Casem, was whipping his Braves into a formidable gridiron fighting machine. The hype surrounding the Alcorn-Valley matchup had been building for weeks, as Alcorn State and Valley State had both marched through the season thus far undefeated. Valley was scheduled to host the Braves, but the press had built the game up to such proportions that the demand for tickets surpassed Valley stadium's capacity. The matchup was moved to Jackson and would be played on a Sunday.

Cooley prepared the Red Devils for battle

It has been said that many a minister of all colors and faiths rushed through church services on that game Sunday, ensuring all were free to make the slated 2:00 p.m. kickoff on time. The stakes could not have been higher. The 1984 SWAC Championship was up for grabs to this game's winner. The Devils were still #1 in the black college poll and were now ranked #4 in the then NCAA Division I-AA poll.

Cooley gives instruction to running back Carl Byrum during the Alcorn-Valley contest

The largest crowd to ever see a sporting event in Mississippi sports history, 63,808 fans, over-packed Mississippi Veterans Memorial Stadium on a sunny day for football. The game was also viewed regionally through the efforts of WLBT-TV, with an estimated 250,000 watching as station sports director Michael Rubinstein and Jackson State head coach W.C. Gordon provided play-by-play commentary. (It is interesting to note here that by halftime of this contest, fans were still trying to get into the game. For safety reasons, the Hinds County fire marshal asked Valley to stop selling tickets, as attendance had already far exceeded the stadium's 62,000-seat capacity. He feared catastrophic results if there was an emergency).

Jam-packed Mississippi Veterans Memorial Stadium. Alcorn vs. Valley

Mississippi Valley's beloved play-by-play announcer, Claiborne Davis, aptly labeled the event the "Game of the Century." Roughly, forty or more press credentials had been requested from Valley's iconic sports information director, Chuck Prophet. Many Division I coaches, as well as several state legislators and congressional representatives, attended the game that afternoon. The collision between Alcorn's much ballyhooed "Soul Patrol" defense and Valley's hugely heralded "Satellite Express" held promise of a showdown to be remembered for all time.

A hard-fought loss to Alcorn

Despite all the preparation for the game, Valley fell by a 42-28 Alcorn victory in the end. This game would become the barometer by which all future games would be compared. In the locker room after the game, Cooley knew he had to get his players ready for the next game, which meant he had to get their minds off this devastating loss. Heartfelt and straightforward, he looked directly in their eyes and said, "I'm proud of each and every one of you; we just played a team that was better prepared.

We were missing key players but even so, the outcome may have been the same had they been here. The game we just played is over and done. Let's go home and get ready for next week. If you carry this game out of here, I promise you we will lose next week also."

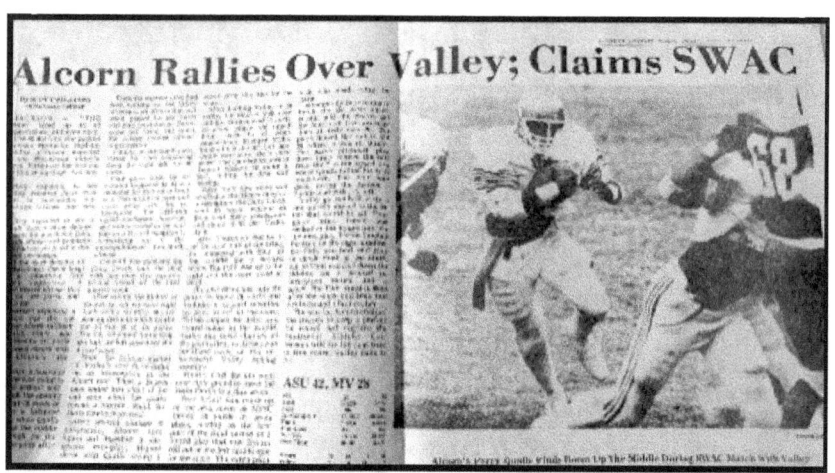

Alcorn wins the SWAC

After the heartbreaking loss to Alcorn State, the Devils rebounded the following week at home. Now 7-1 and no longer atop the black college poll, the Alabama State Hornets, then the newest SWAC members, paid the Devils a visit in Itta Bena. They took a 49-7 a loss back with them to Montgomery.

Valley defeats Alabama State University

The season ended when MVSU hosted the Lions of Langston University. Heading back to Oklahoma from the Devils Den, the Lions took an annihilating 83-11 loss with them.

The Playoffs

Now at season's end, the final 1984 ledger stood 9-1 overall and 5-1 SWAC. Surprising good news greeted the team the following week, when the NCAA invited Coach Cooley and the Devils to participate in the Division I-AA playoffs.

Jerry and Willie, A winning season

It was the first time Mississippi Valley State had ever been invited to play postseason. The team traveled to play the Louisiana Tech Bulldogs in Ruston, Louisiana; but the Devils would lose 66-19.

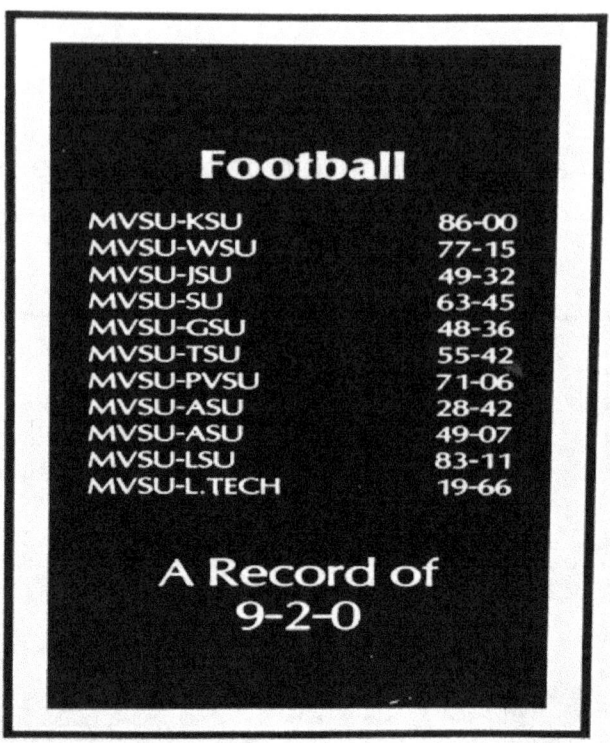

The trophy, Valley's first time participating in an NCAA Championship

To be certain, 1984 was a season for the ages. It was a season that took Mississippi Valley State University, the students, Valley Nation, and the Delta Devils to unimaginable and unprecedented heights. Even further, it took Head Coach Archie "Gunslinger" Cooley to previously unimaginable status as a coach, as it gave him the opportunity, he needed to realize his dream, and in doing so became a LEGEND!

SWAC Domination

The SWAC Legends: Marino Casem, Eddie Robinson, Archie Cooley, and Joe Gibson

Eddie Robinson did not sign Cooley out of high school to play for Grambling because he said he was too small, but things would eventually end up in Cooley's favor as both a player and a coach. In the company of not only Eddie Robinson but also Marino Casem and Joe Gibson, the picture above is worth a thousand words. These were great times for Valley, the Delta Devils, and Cooley. Valley scored more points than any collegiate team during this period, broke several NCAA records, and pushed the envelope so far that the Delta Devils performance gained them nation-wide attention.

Cooley and Jerry

The Red Devils

Red Devils making history

There were many unsung Red Devils behind many of Mississippi Valley's victories. They started out a merry band of players, recruited from the East Coast to the West, down South, and North of the Mason Dixon. Little did they know they too were about to become part of a brotherhood and embark upon a journey that would impact them the rest of their lives.

Red Devils always ready to play

They would become a unit, led by a man who would be forever etched in each one of their memories, Archie "Gunslinger" Cooley. They were Cooley's soldiers, who grew to become a cohesive group after experiencing a grueling, military-style program of blood, sweat, and tears. Realized over time, they would all wear a badge of honor as he brought them together, teaching them how to be men, how to stick together, fight together, and face each opponent together as one. In the end, they would all forever recognize and love each other as brothers. Many fell to the wayside trying to become a part of this war-ready group, this team of boys transformed into men with the same goal of becoming winners in a game they all loved so dearly.

Red Devils Offense

Willie Totten – Satellite – Carrollton, MS
Jerry Rice – World – Crawford, MS
Rodney Hill – Thrill Hill – Atlanta, GA
Carl Byrum – Truck – Southaven, MS
Freddie Parker – Fast Freddie - Heidelberg, MS
Louis Watson – Louis – Mobile, AL
Terry Coleman – TC – Itta Bena, MS
Cleo Armstrong – Cleo – Jackson, MS
Dante Whitaker – Scooter - Atlanta, GA
Maurice Wade – MO – Waldorf, MD
Tony Baker – TB – Louisville, MS
Chris Holmes – Bo-Bo – Mobile, AL
James Thompson – Tom-Tom – Mobile, AL
Lorenzo Clark – Renzo – Clarksdale, MS
Willie Ware – Willie -- Carrollton, MS
Joe Thomas – Tweedy Bird - Baldwin, LA
Jeremiah Snowden – Bull - Bay Minette, AL
Willie Cox – Viking – Clarksdale, MS
Todd Sherman – Todd - New Orleans, LA
Michael Dean – Big Boy – Memphis, TN
Alvin Calhoun – Cal – Monroe, LA
Ray Charles Brown – Ray- Heidelberg, MS
Orlando Hill – Lil Hill – Duck Hill, MS
Roger Totten – Roger – Carrollton, MS
Curtis Debardlebon – BOT – Birmingham, AL
Wilbur Corley – Wilbur – Wesson, MS
Joe Bridges – Joe – Lexington, MS
Thomas Sipp – Sipp – Mobile, AL

Emmitt Mathews – Emmitt – Indianola, MS
Thaddeus Williams – Thad – Yazoo City, MS
Rickey McKenzie – Rickey - Atlanta, GA
Lanford Collins – Lanford - Rosedale, MS
Milton Brooks – Lil Tru - Jackson, MS
Fred Franklin – Freddy – Ellisville, MS
Christopher Haynes – Too Mean – Birmingham, AL
Todd Haygood – Dreamer – Atlanta, GA
Michael Evans – Smooth – Mobile, AL
Harvey Carter – Harvey – French Camp, MS

Red Devils Defense

Tony Haggie – Ram Man – Itta Bena, MS
Roderick Miller – Killa Miller - Tuscaloosa, AL
Daryl Blanks – Blanks – Butler, AL
Darryl Gaines – DG - Mobile, AL
Ricky Tobin – Hyperactive Cat – Bay Minette, AL
Albert Edwards – Al – Mobile, AL
Robert Sanders – Pink Panther -Grenada, MS
Lloyd Mumphrey – FroFro -Memphis, TN
Cleo Green – Cleo – Jackson, MS

Eddie Turner – Turner – Yolk, AL
Clarence Trotter – Dirty Red – Greenville, MS
Jerry Simms – GeeGee – Saginaw, MI
Johnathan Stokes – Stokes – Gaston, AL
Courtney Greer – Greer - St. Louis, MO
Melvin Hollins – Coon – Woodville, MS
Curtis Walker – Hound – Macon, MS
Tyrone Jones – Stiffy - Heidelberg, MS
Boris Ricks – Bo – Los Angeles, CA
Dandre Orey – Orey – Jackson, MS
Walter Liggins – Ligg – Lake Providence, LA
John Murray – John-John – Louisville, MS
Melvin Milligan – Milligan – Waterproof, LA
Aaron Williams – Aaron – Kosciusko, MS
Willie Branch – Cambodia – Cleveland, MS
Dwayne Thomas – DT – Mobile, AL
Willie Nevills – Speedy – Ruleville, MS

Athletic Directors, Trainers, Sports Writers

After the success of the 1983 season, the Mississippi Valley State University Athletic Department was inundated with requests from state and national media outlets for interviews, player profiles, and other media information. First year athletic Director Dr. Joseph Curtis was more than happy to entertain visiting media personnel and give insight into the Valley phenomena that was sweeping the state. So successful had Valley become, its sister schools were casting wary eyes toward Itta Bena, wondering what was going on. Dr. Curtis had the perfect person to handle the onslaught.

Dr. Joseph Curtis,
Athletic Director

Charles "Chuck" Prophet,
Sports Information Director

Valley Sports Information Director, Charles "Chuck" Prophet was a wizard in the public relations department. If anyone could publicize a sports program, he could. He himself was a Valley graduate, and he lived and breathed everything Valley.

Donald Ray Sims,
Asst. Sports Information Director

When the players returned in the summer of 1984, Prophet and his able-bodied assistant, Donald Ray Sims, got down to work. Sims was a natural in this department and worked well with the staff in the athletics department in general. He was knowledgeable and had great chemistry with the players. There was magic in the air, and everyone involved knew that the upcoming season was going to be special.

Also working with Mr. Prophet were two students who knew the outs and ends of Valley Sports. David Linzy and John Martin Branson III were model students and had one thing in common – sports.

John Martin Branson, III and David Linzy

Linzy had been a star athlete in his native Vicksburg, Mississippi, while Branson was a gifted writer. "John-Boy," as Branson lived on campus, was the student newspaper editor-in-chief and active in student life. Both Linzy and Branson became indispensable to the cause that summer, as they became Prophet's right-hand men in many runs between the Devil's Den and the SID's (sports information director) office. That summer also saw Branson acting as an unofficial tutor, helping to guide some of the players in their studies.

It was Prophet and Cooley that laid the basic groundwork for the coach's memorable performance during that summer's SWAC Press Tour. Coach Cooley became the darling of the printed press that season.

TRAINERS
Equipment

No athletic team can function without equipment managers and trainers. Coach Cooley had a lot of faith in his equipment manager. Roy Hutchins who had been a celebrated kicker on the team at one time. After his collegiate career was over, he became a graduate assistant and equipment manager. He was dependable with a sterling reputation, and Coach Cooley knew he had nothing to worry about once those duties were placed in Hutchins' capable hands.

Charles Quinn, Kenneth Gibson, Roy Hutchins, Willie Hickman

Medical

David "Doc" Holt, Head Trainer   Artis Brown, Asst.

David "Doc" Holt and Artis Brown were considered two of the best trainers in the SWAC. Doc Holt was an iconic figure who knew sports medicine and was beloved by athletes. Artis was his able assistant, and they worked very well together. Sore muscles? Sprained Achilles? Have no fear; Doc Holt would soon be there.

NFL Knocking at the Door

Head Coach Bill Walsh invites Cooley, Valley players and coaches to NFL training Camp

Cooley's offensive schemes had piqued the interest of many NFL coaches, announcers, and students of the game. This was no surprise, since Cooley had managed to include many variants to his offense and continued to experiment, learn, and push the envelope far past the norms of college and professional football programs. Cooley was a master, and he knew it. He was not afraid to give anyone a lesson, right there on the spot, because one thing he said was always for sure, "If you don't have the personnel, it won't work anyway."

In his own camp he had a few secret weapons, all of whom he managed to pull in on a shoestring budget. This was a major feat by any measure, but his 1984 team brought the NFL and sports networks, magazines, and newspapers from all over the nation to little Itta Bena, Mississippi, to see Mississippi Valley State University and the Delta Devils. All of this attention by enterprises worth millions was directed at a team that traveled to away games on buses due to the size of its budget.

Jerry Rice, at the time, was setting records and profiled in the November 1983 issue of Sports Illustrated with an article titled, "He's the Catch of the Year." He finished the season with an I-AA record of 102 catches and 1,475 yards.

Forty Niner's Coach Bill Walsh and Archie Cooley

Rice brought excitement to the 49ers camp, especially after winning the MVP in the Blue-Gray game. After receiving Bill Walsh's nod of approval, he was the 16th pick drafted by the 49ers in 1985.

Cooley's spread offense was a hit across both college and NFL football, while some of the more conservative coaches deemed it too gimmicky for their program. Although no one in the NCAA or the NFL would give him credit for his innovative approach, that did not matter to the Gunslinger. He set his own path and walked his own way. As he would say, "That is mighty fine by me!"

After all the attention Cooley brought to Mississippi Valley, NFL teams via Draft or Free Agency picked up hosts of players from his 1984 team. They include: Jerry Rice (San Francisco 49ers), Willie Totten (Buffalo Bills), Vincent Brown (New England Patriots), Aaron Williams (New England Patriots), Dante Whitaker (New York Giants), Lloyd Mumphrey (San Francisco 49ers), Darryl Gaines (Kansas City Chiefs), Joe Thomas (Denver Broncos), Rodrick Miller (Atlanta Falcons), Robert Sanders (New York Jets), Curtis Debardlebon (Houston Gamblers), Carl Byrum (Buffalo Bills), Louis Watson (Cleveland Browns) and Freddie Parker (Green bay Packers).

AFTER THE VALLEY

After leaving the Valley in 1986, Cooley became the head coach at Arkansas Pine Bluff one year prior to the university move into the Southwestern Athletic Conference (SWAC). Cooley coached there for four years and served as the athletic director and an associate professor.

Cooley became the head coach at Norfolk State University in 1993, but only served in the position for one year. After Norfolk, Cooley put down his coaching hat to regroup and get in some quality time with his family.

Coaching remained Cooley's passion, and in 2000, he began hearing the call again as he accepted the head coaching job at Paul Quinn College, and NAIA member trying to establish a new program. Cooley built this program and remained head coach until 2006.

Cooley was inducted into the SWAC Hall of Fame in 2007. The word "legend" is tossed around quite a bit these days. However, there are many instances when the word truly applies to an individual who has made a significant impact in a given field. Their contributions are so extraordinarily important, that to ignore them would be an oversight of the highest order.

Cooley retires with many successes in sports and in life

In the ever-tough world of coaching football, one must be exceptionally gifted to have the words "legend" or "legendary" affixed next to their name. This is especially true in the rough and tumble world of black college coaching. Archie "Gunslinger" Cooley was never a man to back down from a challenge. He was feared and loathed but beloved and admired by the national sports world and an entire college nation of fans. What he did at Mississippi Valley State University remains, to this day, an unprecedented feat in Valley's 67-year football history.

Cooley's departure from Mississippi Valley signaled the end of an era in Delta Devil football. Never since has a coach taken Valley football to such heights. By sheer stubborn desire, Coach Cooley brought a team from mediocre to national promise. His offensive plays had mouths wide open for three memorable seasons, and word of his offensive wizardry spread everywhere. Never afraid or leery of the press, he rarely missed an interview. He became the darling of the media and preached Valley. He made Mississippi Valley State's sister schools sit up and take notice.

Mississippi Valley State University's Department of Athletics hosts an annual Trailblazers Gala to honor those who paved the way for the current MVSU administration and student-athletes. Cooley received the Trailblazer award in 2017 recognizing his accomplishments and contributions to Mississippi Valley State University.

MVSU President Jerryl Briggs presents the 2017 Trailblazer Award to Cooley, Rice and Totten.

Cooley was also recognized by MVSU in September 2018. He was honored by the school with the team field house renamed after him. It was a recognition that brought tears to his and his family's eyes.

Delta Devils field house and training facility was renamed in his honor in September 2018

In the spring of 2017, former Valley Red Devils Clarence Trotter, Cleo Armstrong, Brian Williams, and Darryl Gaines surprised Cooley with a Red Devils jersey. He was visibly moved and honored by the recognition.

Brian Williams, Cleo Armstrong, Clarence Trotter, and Darryl Gaines

With stints at the University of Arkansas at Pine Bluff and Virginia Union at Richmond, Virginia, Cooley's aura and reputation for winning made him a living black college legend. What had taken some of the great black college coaches' decades to build on the gridiron, Cooley took only three seasons to build. His coaching style and extraordinary playbook found him in great demand.

When the iconic Bill Walsh of the NFL's San Francisco 49ers came calling about the Delta Devils offensive scheme of things, the 49ers front office sent for him. Who is going to turn an opportunity like that? No one! What an honor. All things considered, he's unequivocally one of the greatest college football coaches ever. In three short years, he accomplished more than what other coaches could ever hope to achieve.

In retirement, he is still sought out for interviews and maybe a football camp or two. He is humbled and so appreciative for all the accolades and honors bestowed upon him. A more fitting tribute was headed his way in December 2018. It would be one of his crowning moments.

Archie "Gunslinger" Cooley

At the College Football Hall of Fame in Atlanta, Georgia, on December 6, 2018, before a room full of invited guests from the college football world and a nationally televised ESPN-TV audience of millions, this legendary figure was nationally recognized for his enduring contributions to college football through the HBCU network of colleges and universities. He received the coveted NCFAA's (National College Football Awards Association) Contributions to Football Award. This award is given to coaches and players who have made great contributions to and who have influenced college football in America.

Coach & Mrs. Cooley arriving at awards presentation in Atlanta...

In the ever-tough world of coaching football, one must be exceptionally gifted to have the words "legend" or "legendary" affixed next to their name. This is especially true in the rough and tumble world of black college coaching. Archie "Gunslinger" Cooley was never a man to back down from a challenge. He was feared and loathed but beloved and admired by the national sports world and an entire college nation of fans. What he did at Mississippi Valley State University remains, to this day, an unprecedented feat in Valley's 67-year football history.

Coach Cooley's heralded Satellite Offense is still used today and is now known in NFL circles as the West Coast Offense. Pointed out by award presenter/ESPN football analyst Jay Walker, the late great San Francisco 49er's Coach Bill Walsh was so intrigued by the offense that he sent for Coach Cooley to come west and teach it to him.

Cooley (and former Alcorn legend Marino Casem) on stage at awards ceremony...

During his impressive coaching career, Coach Cooley even went up against two figures who were already legends at the time in black college football. In 1983, in a classic gridiron thriller in Memphis at the Liberty Bowl, Coach Cooley humbled Tennessee State and Coach "Big John" Merritt (his mentor and collegiate coach), 51-38. He would go on to eclipse another giant (Grambling State's Eddie Robinson) a year later in Indianapolis' first Circle City Classic, 48-36. Redemption had come at last.

Cooley at long last: A nationally recognized college football icon and a true legend

Finally, redeeming grace found Coach Cooley. Those of us who were present and attending Valley in the early 1980s had front row seats to his greatness, and we are so proud for his shining moment. He received his proper acknowledgment, and watching him receive it on the national sports stage before millions of TV viewers made it all the sweeter. As long as MVSU exists, his achievements will stand permanently with a great institution.

EPILOGUE

On February 1, 1950, an icy cold winter day, the governor of Mississippi, Fielding Wright, in the company of Dr. James Herbert White and other dignitaries, assembled on a desolate piece of land about a mile from Itta Bena. That afternoon, ground was broken for the future home of Mississippi Valley State University, then to be called Mississippi Vocational College. Dr. White had been selected by the Mississippi Legislature to serve as its first president. He had given up the presidency of the historical HBCU, Lane College at Jackson, Tennessee, to take on the monumentally herculean task of building a university in the heart of the Mississippi Delta – the middle of a cotton patch.

No one at the time could ever have envisioned the sport of football bringing this university the unparalleled glory it did. Had he lived long enough, I am convinced Dr. White would have not only shaken Coach Archie "Gunslinger" Cooley's hand, but would have made Valley State Cooley's permanent home base.

Cooley's was one of the most innovative football minds of our generation. He is now, after 40 years of coaching, ranked high up with his football contemporaries. When the Southwestern Athletic Conference is mentioned in conversation these days, Cooley's name is spoken in the same breath as Eddie Robinson, Jake Gaither, Ace Mumford and Marino Casem. His genius at offensive play calling and offensive scheming led to the National Football League using their version of Cooley's genius, the West Coast Offense, for years now.

On October 21, 2017, bers of the 1984 team assembled at Mississippi Valley State University to be recognized. It had been 33 years since these guys had been in one room together, and it was a Red Devils reunion of historic proportions. Teammates together one more time; what a blessing it was!

STATS

Cooley has a rich and broad coaching background.

Biographical details	
Born	March 18, 1939 (age 80) Sumrall, Mississippi
Playing career	
1960	Jackson State
Position(s)	Center, linebacker
Coaching career	
1964–1970	Southside HS (MS)
1971–1973	Alcorn State (DL/LB)
1974–1979	Tennessee State (LB)
1980–1986	Mississippi Valley State (HC)
1987–1990	Arkansas–Pine Bluff (HC)
1993-1994	Norfolk State (HC)
2000–2006	Paul Quinn (HC)
Head coaching record	
Overall	83–78–5 (college)
Bowls	0–1 (NCAA D-I-AA playoffs) MVSU

AWARDS

SWAC Co-Coach of the Year 1980

SWAC Coach of the Year 1983

JSU Hall of Fame 1986

All-American Football Foundation
Johnny Vaught Lifetime Achievement Award 2000

SWAC Hall of Fame 2002*

MVSU Hall of Fame 2007

SWAC Hall of Fame 2007

SWAC Lifetime Achievement Award 2010

JSU Hall of Fame/Player of the Century (Center) 2011

Oak Park High Hall of Fame 2012

MVSU Trailblazer Award 2017

National College Football Awards Association
'Contributions to Football Award' 2018

Life Member SWAC Football Coach

PHOTO GALLERY
MEMORIAL

With a heartfelt tone, Cooley remembers stories of each of his players from when he recruited them through all the time he coached them. He has many fond memories of the players who have gone on to meet with God as his heart weighs heavy thinking and talking about them. They were his sons, my boys, as he would call them in an endearing voice.

Clockwise From Right: Vincent Goode, Gregory Hodo, Gary Bush, Bruce McAllister, Otis Culliver, Clarence Alexander, Willie Breauxsaus, James Thompson, Melvin Milligan, Tony Haggie, Harvey Carter, Christopher Haynes, Ricky Hatten, Sam Harris, Willie Green, Guy Forrest

Not Pictured: Cleo Green, James Stovall

Cooley's younger brother, Lloyd, also served his country.
He has also gone on to be with God.

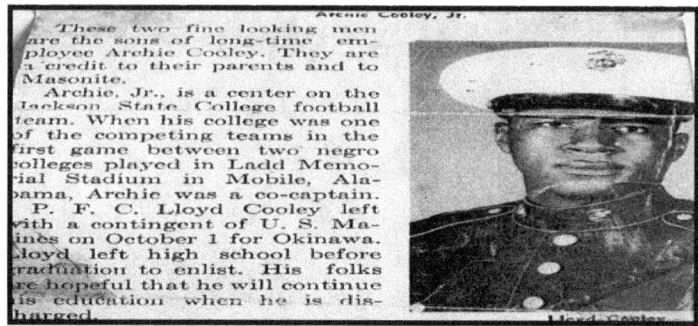

Players and Fans

Who you gonna call? SWAC Busters!!

Cleo Armstrong, Willie Totten and Curtis DeBardlabon believe too

MILITARY DAYS

Prairie View Wins 24-12 Over Tigers

A first period score and a field goal and two more touchdowns in the third quarter gave the Prairie View Panthers a 24-12 victory over a stubborn Jackson State College here Saturday night.

Panther halfback Sam Clark skirted left end for ten yards and the first period Prairie View score and led 7-0 at halftime following John Harris' first of three conversions.

Harris then added a 20-yard field goal in the third period with Archie Seals and Carl Jackson also scoring for the Panthers. Seals' score was on a one yard plunge and Jackson toured around right end for 15-yards and his tally. Harris added two more Pat's.

Jackson State scoring came late in the fourth period when Tiger center, Archie Cooley intercepted a stray Panther pass and raced 55-yards for the six-pointer. Later a pass from Roy Curry to Cornelius Addison carried for 31-yards and a score. Both attempts at conversions failed.

Oilers' Line Coach Comes With Record

HEIDELBERG— Archie Cooley, Jr., line coach of Heidelberg High School, is a native of Jones County, having gone to Oak Park High School in Laurel. He is a graduate of Jackson State College and received his B. S. degree in 1961.

He played football and baseball at Jackson State and made all conference in both sports. Also he played football in the armed services and made all-Army at Guard in 1963.

Coach Cooley has worked at Southside High School, six years where he has a record of 173 wins and 10 losses in girls' basketball, winning two girls' State Over-All Championships in 1966 and 1967. He also coached the boys track team to the State Championship in class A last year.

He is married to the former Georgia Reed of Belzoni, Miss and they are the parents of two children a boy and a girl. They are members of St. Paul Methodist Church in Laurel, Miss.

At Ft. Devens, Mass.

Ft. Bragg Football Dragons Begin 1963 Season Sunday

By Lt. James L. Turner, Jr.

...ted with two "first" teams ...elect from, Coach A. L. ...tton leads his Ft. Bragg ...gons into their first season ...gridiron play this week when ...ey meet Ft. Devens, Mass., ...n an East Coast Interservice Conference (ECIC) game.

Referring to his squads simply as "X" and "Y," Coach Stratton has the pleasant task of calling upon two elevens that are filled to the brim with talent that will make the enemy look twice, if not a third time. Ft. Bragg, leaving the confines of intra-post play, will field a club that is sprinkled with collegiate All-Americans and several veterans of military service ball. With an 11 game schedule on tap, Coach Stratton hopes to see his single wing attack produce the same results as his 1961 and '62 post championship clubs.

The Ft. Devens team has its work cut out this Sunday afternoon as, Ft. Bragg opens its season on the road.

The brightest spot on the '63 squad is definitely the backfield, with eyes focused on the fullback and tailback spots. Slated to work in the backfield of the "X" group, is a seasoned combination of 5'-11", 220 pound fullback Wayne Nichols (MB, 325); 6'-0", 190 pound tailback Paul Flint (Hq, 504), and 5'-11", 198 pound slotback Chanks Thomas (D, 325). Thomas and Nichols played for Stratton last season where their speed produced a fiery wide-open attack. Quarterbacking the club is Eldon Perdew (C, 504), a 1962 graduate of West Point.

The spotlight in the "Y" backfield is on fullback Al Rushatz (C, 505), a '62 All-East, Honorable Mention All-American and Coaches All-American from West Point. The 5'-10" Rushatz will be flanked by an equally potent backfield ace, Ed Shaw (82nd Med). Shaw, a 5'-11", 200 pound '61 graduate of the University of Pennsylvania, will fill in at tailback. Slotback duties go to 6'-1", 212 pound Jim Scurry (82nd Med.), a veteran of eight years on the military gridiron.

Lacking the experience but just as adept as his counterpart Perdew, quarterback reins on the "Y" squad will go to 5'-11", 176 pound Grady Lee Jones (C, 503 MP). Jones played ball last season in Korea.

The Dragons can look at their line with justified pride, where two college All-Americans will add additional experience.

Standing at guard on the "X" club are 5'-11" John Godbolt (D, 501) and 6'-0" Archie Cooley (C, 92nd Arty), both Small College All-American linemen. Godbolt is a '60 All-SIAC graduate of Morris Brown College, Atlanta, Ga., and Cooley is a '61 All-Conference grad from Jackson State College, Jackson, Miss. Both men weigh in at 205.

Experience is also the key word at the guard slot on the "Y" team. A five-year veteran of military play, Roosevelt Boykins (C, 504) tips the scales at 197 with Ed Davis (C, 501) weighing in at 205. Davis has eight years of military play under his belt.

Tackle slots on the "X" team will be filled by 210 pound John Sinkovitz (B, 325) and 2?? pound Leroy Ferguson. "Y" members at tackle include 6'-0" Michael Casp (MB, 50?) and 6'-4" Lawrence Olds (H 320th Arty). Casp, a '62 graduate of West Point, captained the Cadet eleven in 1961. Olds is a '62 graduate of Nor

Prep Talk

By PHIL WALLACE
Daily News Sports Writer

Heidelberg Southside Cagers Hold 152-4 Record For 4 Years

You better sit down before hearing this.

Here's a basketball team which has won 65 games in a row. That's right, 65 games without defeat and there's no telling when it will lose. Some say never.

The Southside High girls of Heidelberg are the young ladies we're talking about and their coach is a guy named Archie Cooley whose record is nothing short of phenomenal.

Not only has Cooley led the Southside Bravettes to 65 straight victories, but consider, for a moment, the man's four-year record of 152-4.

Southside High won the State girls' championship last year beating Jackson Lanier at the Mississippi Coliseum here.

And, with a string of 20 straight wins this season, chances are better than good that the Bravettes will return to the throne.

Cooley took over as head coach at Southside in 1964 and proceeded to lead the team to a 44-3 record losing only to Quitman Owens, twice, and once to Ellisville.

In 1965-66, Southside had a 43-1 record losing only to Jackson Jim Hill and last season, no one, not anybody, beat the Bravettes as they marched to a 45-0 record.

The prime reason for Southside's success on the offensive side is Ella Mae Faulkner who is averaging over 37 points per game with 657 already chalked up this season.

Mary Jones is hitting 19.2 per game with Mary Thomas 11 per game and Jerry Pierce 11.3. Defensive leaders, who Cooley says are the keys to his program, include Martha Clayton, Dot Barnett and Fay Dukes.

Southside has gone over the 100-point mark in three games this season. And that's in 28 minutes of play, as girls play seven-minute quarters.

The club is averaging 76.7 points per game and won their last game, 100-24, Wednesday night.

"I believe the success to my program is good defense," says Cooley. "We play a man-to-man type defense and try to keep the basketball as much as possible."

Cooley says the ball is usually on Southside's end of the floor "about 85 percent of the time" giving the opposition little chance to score.

"This is my philosophy, keeping the ball as much as possible, then playing tough defense when the other team gets it."

Cooley also said his junior high program was very good allowing the younger girls to be introduced to basketball at an early age.

The Southside boys team, under Coach Jerry Redmond, is doing OK, too. The Braves are -2 now, but the Bravettes are the talk of the town.

Friday, Nov. 18, 1960 State Times, Jackson, Miss.

Fighting Jackson Tigers Come Off Backs And Win

The Lethal Ground Attack Jells As Merritt Foresaw

By CECIL WALTON
State Times Staff Writer

Having scrambled off their backs, fought through the chaos of early season defeats and muscled their way back among the best of the crack Southwestern Conference, the Tiger Cats of Jackson State land at Alumni field Saturday on the winning wings of five and three.

They will lock horns with the Steers of Tyler, Texas and could possibly come out of the scrimmage with a Conference clause of better than 500.

If this be the case, the ferocious Felines of Big John Merritt will have proved again that it's not the way you begin — but the way you end.

Can they take the Texans?

They can take the Texans.

After all the push, pull and shove, the big Cats are definitely with those at the head of the line. They got up, fought back and took their rightful place. By doing so, they gave statute to the prediction Big John made when he said, "It's a good team and it'll jell by mid-season."

And jell it did. Following their humiliation at the hands of Southern U, the Tigers Cats swung back into the midst of their conference foes with such sawbucking fury that they wound up in the first division.

Accounting for this great surge ahead was a multiple diagnosis by Merritt and his crew, and the coming-into-their-own of freshman halfback Chico Jordan, who ground out 150 yards against Wiley, Lewis, McRea, who terrorized his way into Red Baker's fullback slot and the manipulation of Willie Richardson in the backfield and Jake Greer at end.

Part of the multiple diagnosis engaged in by Merritt was his ability to realize what he had— and play it to the hilt.

Early in the season he realized all he had was the larruping arm

Another advantage of Richardson being in the backfield is his ability to turn loose the long pass. A pitch-out, Addison to Richardson, could draw in the linebackers, leaving Jake Greer clean. Greer has snagged 10 aerials.

Cornelius Addison has chunked over 1000 yards of passes this season and is currently leading the conference in total offense, as well as passing. He is double danger when he tosses the ball.

The Tigers defense is anchored by a hard - driving fast - moving center named Archie Cooley, a linebacker deluxe. Cooley has been such a terror this season that he is easily considered one of, if not the best, middle men in the conference.

Corner men behind the line are very much improved on defending the short pass and run plays. This improvement is the result of changes made as the season followed.

Looking extra good is 240 pound, six feet three inch tackle James Hayes who is already being called "pro timber."

The Tigers will guard their goal with what Merritt calls "Our looping defense."

Merritt will probably need his "looping defense" come Saturday afternoon.

Although the Texans don't boast an impressive won - lost as the Tigers, the Steers are a potential team, capable of exploding at the drop of a spark.

They bring with them a great off-tackle halfback who is the leading ground gainer in the conference. This boy could mean embarrassment for the Tigers, if their defense can't hold him in check, and the Steers will leave town with Jackson State buried deep in the second division of the Conference.

This is a must game for the Tigers because of that. If they win it they ride high with Southern and Prairie View.

Saturday is Band Day for Jackson State. As an added attraction

Players Battle For Team Berths

JACKSON, Miss. — Coach John A. Merritt, headman of the Jackson State college Tigers, sent his squad through a lengthy workout Saturday as the Bengals closed their second week of rigorous training. The two-a-day practice sessions ended Monday as classes were scheduled to begin Tuesday.

Competition for starting berths has been more terrific this season than during any season since Merritt took over as head coach six years ago; in fact, competition for a spot in the 33-man squad has left little to be desired except possibly room for four or five more men.

Tiger Albert Jackson, a sophomore from Clarksdale where he played high school football at Higgins High, made it easy for the Tiger coaching staff to agree on shifting Archie Cooley, who also played fullback as a freshman, to center. Cooley, a big, strong body of willingness and determination, is pushing his city mate, Reader Jordan, for the starting assignment. The decision to shift Cooley to the pivotal post had an additional advantage in that it allowed the Tiger coaches to leave Aaron Jones at end.

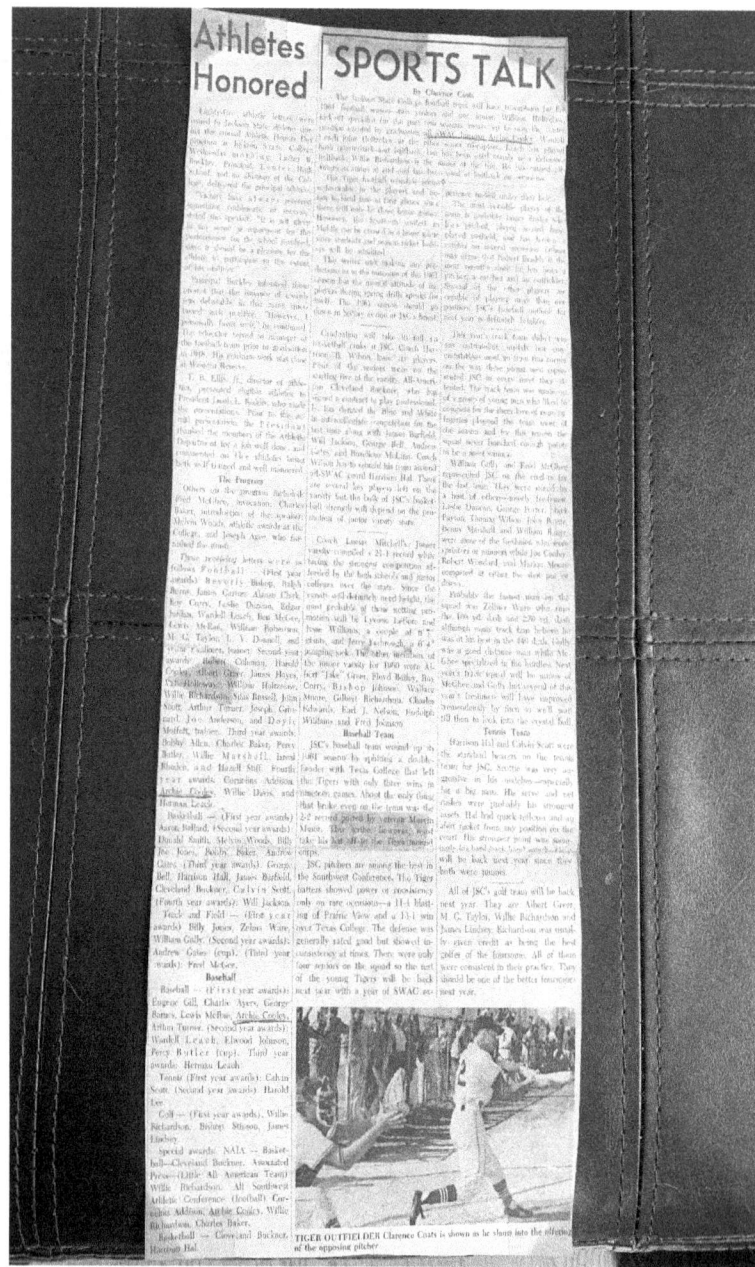

NEGRO NEWS OF INTEREST
By MRS. HATTIE V. J. McINNIS, Editor
Telephone 426-9937

IMPERIAL GOSPEL SINGERS

The program which was to be rendered by the Imperial Gospel Singers was postponed, from Friday night Sept. 13, to Friday night, Sept. 20. The public is invited, including all the gospel singers of this city.

IN MEMORY

In loving memory of Albert McGowan, who departed this life September 14, 1960.

Three years have passed since the Lord took you from us. Just around the corner, a little out of sight. You went ahead into Eternal Light.

Sadly missed by,
Mrs. Mattie McGowan, Wife
Mrs. Mattie Harper, Daughter, and Grandchildren

ARCHIE COOLEY, GUARD

When Fort Bragg's football Dragons begin the 1963 season a Laurelite, Archie Cooley, will be in the line-up as guard. Archie, (C, 92nd Arty.) is an Oak Park graduate and a '61 All-Conference graduate from Jackson State College. He weighs 205 pounds.

JACKSON STATE-PRAIRIE VIEW

Jackson State opens against the Prairie View Panthers Sept. 21 at Prairie View. Since the Texans have been picked by two writers to capture conference Laurels this season, the Tigers will get a king-size test in their first outing. Jackson, incidentally, isn't included in the top four picks.

In Edgar "Chico" Jordan, 180-pound speedster from Laurel, and Leslie Duncan, 185-pound Tuscaloosa, Ala. native who runs like an antelope, Jackson State probably has the best one-two punch in Negro collegiate circles. A supporting cast includes Taft Reed, 197-pound back from Hattiesburg; Gloster Richardson, 195-pound from Greenville; Elbert Vaughn, 182-pound; Hattiesburg; Otis Spann, 201-pound from Jackson; Bennie Crenshaw, Mobile, Alabama; Tellis B. Ellis III, of Jackson, and about three freshman backs, will keep the Jackson State opposition honest.

Persons familiar with the 1962 squad will miss Harold Cooley of Laurel. Foxy "Ox" the wily Texan with the Missouri philosophy, (show me) will get a good chance to pass judgment on the Tiger's offense and defense Saturday.

NEW FACULTY MEMBERS

Among the new faculty members beginning work this year are the following teachers: Mrs. Jennie Rose Carter, languages; Louis Miles, Study Hall Supervisor; Mrs. Armendia Young, English; Miss Edwina Currie, Second Grade; Mrs. Gloria Chess, Sixth Grade; Miss Gladys Washington, Fourth Grade; Miss Jewell Crawford, Social Studies, Oak Park Jr.-Sr. High School; Miss Nancy Ellis, First Grade, Miss Jettie P. Evans, First Grade, Nora Davis Elementary; Miss Francis Frazier, Sixth Grade, Miss Elizabeth Dean, First Grade, Sandy Gavin Elementary School.

CHARTER RENTALS INSTRUCTION
HESLER-NOBLE AIR SERVICE
MUNICIPAL HANGER
Laurel Airport—Dial 428-4653

CONTRIBUTORS

INTERVIEWS

Archie "Gunslinger" Cooley

Dwight Cooley

Lisa Cooley

Mrs. Georgia Cooley

Betty McCarthy

COOLEY'S PHOTO GALLERY

Roderick Miller

John Branson

Valley Yearbook Staff

COOLEY'S MILITARY DAYS

Lisa Cooley

Mrs. Georgia Cooley

COOLEY'S NEWS ARTICLES

Lisa Cooley

Jackson Dailey News

Mississippi State Times

Heidelberg News

LA Times

Chicago Tribune

Monroe News-Star-World

www.ingramcontent.com/pod-product-compliance
Lightning Source LLC
Chambersburg PA
CBHW081400070526
44583CB00020B/2609